CONDITIONING FOR
Basketball

Matt Brzycki • Shaun Brown

A Division of Howard W. Sams & Co.

Published by Masters Press (A Division of Howard W. Sams & Co.)
2647 Waterfront Parkway E. Dr.
Suite 300
Indianapolis, IN 46214

Published 1993.

Printed in the United States of America

Library of Congress Cataloging-in-Publication Data
  Brzycki, Matt, 1957-
      Conditioning for basketball / Matt Brzycki and Shaun Brown.
          p. cm.
      Includes bibliographical references (p.).
      ISBN 0-940279-56-8 :
      1. Basketball–training. 2. Weight training. 3. Physical education and training.
  I. Brown, Shaun, 1964- . II. Title.
  GV885.35.B79   1993
  796.323'07–dc20   993-15176
                                                                              CIP

Front cover photos provided by Simon Griffiths (upper left), Ted Lambrinides
(upper right), the University of Kentucky Sports Information Department (lower
right), and Joel Blunk (lower left).

Back cover photo provided by the University of Kentucky Sports Information
Department.

Cover design by Christy Pierce.

"The first principle on which the game (of basketball) was based was that it should demand of, and develop in, the player the highest type of physical and athletic development."

Dr. James Naismith
May 1914

To all of my family and friends for their many years of support.

—Shaun Brown

To Alicia Grimaldi and our future together.

—Matt Brzycki

TABLE OF CONTENTS

ACKNOWLEDGEMENTS

The authors would like to express their sincere gratitude to these individuals for their contributions in the making of this book.

Joel Blunk, the Strength Coach of the Vanderbilt University Men's and Women's Basketball Teams, for providing photographs.

Ed Cicale, the Strength Coach of Oak Hills High School (Ohio), for furnishing photographs.

Sandra Boyken, Chris Cameron and Susan Hazzard of the University of Kentucky Sports Information Department for their patience and assistance.

JoAnn Hauser, the Athletic Trainer for the University of Kentucky Men's Basketball Team for reviewing sections of the manuscript.

Kurt Kehl and Donna Nebbia of the Princeton University Office of Athletic Communications for providing photographs from their files.

Dr. Ted Lambrinides, the Director of Research of Hammer Strength, Incorporated, for furnishing photographs of Hammer equipment.

The Providence College Sports Information Department for providing a photograph from their files.

Jim Small for lending insight into strength and conditioning from his many years of experience at the scholastic, collegiate and professional levels.

Amy Stoneman of Nautilus (Virginia) for supplying photographs of Nautilus equipment.

Resa Wright of the University of Kentucky for taking photographs.

Holly Kondras of Masters Press, our in-house editor.

Tony Alexander, Aaron Beth, Tom Boyd, Delray Brooks, Rich Burton, John Carlson, Christopher Colbeck, Rob Dribbon, David Metzbower, Todd Milholland, Katie Mottram, Tom O'Rourke, Sasha Ruiz, Ed Spatola, Michele Spreen, Greg Williams and Shane Woolf who appeared throughout the book as demonstrators in the photographs relating to specific exercises.

Finally, the authors would like to acknowledge all of the coaches and educators who have enlightened, encouraged and inspired them over the years.

PHOTO CREDITS

All photos by Matt Brzycki except those on pages 12 and 76 provided by the University of Kentucky Sports Information Department, on pages 15 (bottom) and 154 by Shaun Brown, on pages 72, 99 and 145 provided by the Princeton University Office of Athletic Communications, on page 88 by Resa Wright, on page 92 by David Coyle, and on page 142 by Thomas F. Maguire.

All photos in chapters three and ten used to illustrate exercises are also by Matt Brzycki with the exception of the following.

PG	PHOTO	CREDIT
27	Leg Press - Nautilus	Nautilus (VA)
28	Hip Abduction - Nautilus	Joel Blunk
30	Leg Curl - Manual Resistance	Resa Wright
33	Dorsi Flexion - Plate-loading	Resa Wright
34	Bench Press - Nautilus	Nautilus (VA)
36	Decline Press - Plate-loading	Ed Cicale
37	Bent Arm Fly - Nautilus	Nautilus (VA)
42	Pullover - Plate-loading	Nautilus (VA)
47	Bent Over Raise - Plate-loading	Resa Wright
53	Wrist Extension - Manual Resistance	Resa Wright
54	Situp - Manual Resistance	Shaun Brown
54	Situp - Nautilus	Nautilus (VA)
131	Standing Forward "V"	Shaun Brown
132	Standing Lateral "V"	Shaun Brown
133	Groin Stretch	Shaun Brown
134	"Saigon" Squat	Shaun Brown
135	Knee Pull	Shaun Brown
136	Crossover	Shaun Brown
137	"Quad" Stretch	Resa Wright
138	Shooter's Stretch	Resa Wright
139	Standing Calf	Shaun Brown
140	Wall Walk	Shaun Brown

FOREWORD

It's hard to believe that basketball was invented over 100 years ago. In 1891, Dr. James Naismith got two peach baskets from a janitor. He then hung these baskets in a 35 x 45 foot gymnasium at the YMCA Training School in Springfield, Massachusetts, and "basket" ball was born. Little did he know that his new game would develop into one of the most popular and widely-known sports in the world.

The original game differed markedly from the way it's played today. In it's infancy, basketball was played by two teams of 9 men each. The players threw a soccer ball into a peach basket. When a team scored, one player had to climb a ladder to remove the ball from the basket. It sure seems a long way from today's March Madness!

Back in the early days of basketball, weightlifting was done almost exclusively by professional weightlifters and circus strongmen. Needless to say, weightlifting was simply not done by the average person or, for that matter, even by the athletes. Fears of lost flexibility, dulled reactions and ruined skills were the prevalent notion. Over the years, competitive weightlifting gradually evolved into more specialized weight training — or strength training — programs. Knowledgeable individuals were soon hired to develop and administer these programs and became known as strength coaches. Today, strength training has been accepted by men and women of all ages in virtually every sport, including basketball.

At the University of Kentucky, strength training for basketball has come a long way as well. When I first arrived here, the strength facility for basketball consisted of a few Nautilus machines located in a gloomy area under the concourse in Memorial Coliseum. That weight room has been transformed into a gleaming, multi-million dollar facility that is overflowing with the latest strength and conditioning tools that are available. Our present facility for basketball compares to few others in the country.

As a coach, I appreciate my players' results from a safe and efficient strength and conditioning program. Here at the University of Kentucky – and before with the New York Knicks and at Providence College – I've felt very strongly about the importance of strength and conditioning as a way of preventing injury and improving a player's potential to excel. The strides that our basketball program has made in the past three years are truly remarkable and are due, in part, to our mandatory strength and conditioning program. I also recognize the fact that training a basketball player like a competitive weightlifter is a terrible mistake. For this reason, we don't have any bench press meets or bodybuilding contests — there's no "maxing out" and no posedowns by our players. Nor do we do any activities that might invite injury, such as explosive lifting. That's why it's necessary to obtain appropriate advice and information about strength and conditioning from reliable sources.

Winning games is a result of dedication and preparation. Total preparation for basketball is a combination of the activities that are performed on the court, in the classroom and in the weightroom.

Rick Pitino
Head Basketball Coach
The University of Kentucky

THE FIRST HALF:

INCREASING FUNCTIONAL STRENGTH

1 YOUR MUSCLES: WHERE THEY ARE AND HOW THEY WORK

Before beginning any detailed discussions about strength and conditioning for basketball, it's necessary to understand some basic anatomy and muscular function. Your body is basically a system of levers. Movement of these levers (your bones) is produced by your muscles. Incredible as it may seem, there are more than 600 muscles in the human body, each of which is comprised of numerous muscle fibers which, in turn, are made up of many myofibrils. (To get an idea of this arrangement, picture a telephone cable containing hundreds of wires.) In fact, each of your forearms alone is made up of 19 separate muscles with such exotic-sounding names as "extensor carpi radialis brevis" and "flexor digitorum superficialis." However, it's well beyond the scope and purpose of this book to discuss your muscles in such great detail. Instead, this introductory chapter will focus on only your major muscle groups – muscles that you should have a working knowledge of as a coach or an athlete.

The major muscle groups described will be the hips, legs, upper torso, arms, abdominals and lower back. These 6 major muscle groups are further subdivided into their most important components. Brief notes on each muscle's location and function are given along with terminology that is generally accepted in weight room parlance.

HIPS

Buttocks

Your buttocks muscles are the largest and strongest muscles in your body. The buttocks are composed of 3 main muscle groups: the gluteus maximus, the gluteus medius and the gluteus minimus. The primary functions of the "glutes" are hip extension (driving your upper leg backward) and hip abduction (spreading your legs apart). The buttocks are important muscles used in most basketball skills such as running down the court, crashing the boards, leaping to block a shot, performing your jump shot and jamming the ball through the hoop. In addition, the gluteus medius is used when you shuffle your feet from side to side.

3

Adductors

The adducter group is composed of 5 muscles that are located throughout your inner thigh. These inner thigh muscles are used during adduction of the hip (bringing your legs together). On the courts, your adductors are used as stabilizers when you are down in a good defensive position and when you shuffle your feet from side to side.

Iliopsoas

This is a collective term for the primary muscles of your front hip area – the iliacus and the psoas. The main function of the iliopsoas is to flex your hip (bring your knee to your chest). Your iliopsoas plays a major role in many skills like lifting your knees as you run and raising your lead leg when you lay the ball up into the bucket. The iliacus and the psoas are sometimes considered with the muscles of the abdomen.

LEGS

Hamstrings

Your "hams" are located on the backside of your upper leg and actually include 3 separate muscles: the semimembranosus, the semitendinosus and the biceps femoris. Together, these muscles are involved in flexing the lower leg around the knee joint (raising your heel toward your hip). The hams are used during virtually all running and jumping activities. Unfortunately, the muscle is very susceptible to pulls and tears. Strong hamstrings are necessary to balance the effects of the powerful quadricep muscles.

Quadriceps

Your "quads" are the most important muscles on the front part of your thighs. As the name suggests, your quadriceps are made up of 4 muscles: the vastus lateralis, the vastus intermedius, the vastus medialis and the rectus femoris. The main function of your quads is extending (or straightening) your lower leg at the knee joint. Like the hams, the quads are also involved in just about all running and jumping skills.

Calves

Each calf is made up of two important muscles – the gastrocnemeus (or "gastroc") and the soleus – which are located on the backside of your lower leg. Your calves are involved when your foot is extended at your ankle (or when you rise on your toes). The calves play a major role in running and jumping activities.

Dorsi Flexors

The front part of your lower leg contains 4 muscles which are sometimes simply referred to as the "dorsi flexors." The largest of these muscles is the tibialis anterior. Your dorsi flexors are primarily used in flexing your foot toward your knee. It is critical to strengthen the dorsi flexors as a safeguard against shin splints.

UPPER TORSO

Chest

The major muscle surrounding your chest area is the pectoralis major. Your "pecs" pull your upper arm down and across your body. Like most of your upper torso muscles, your pecs are involved in rebounding, shot blocking, shooting and passing skills.

Back

Your latissimus dorsi is the long, broad muscle that comprises most of your upper back. Your "lats" are the largest muscles in your upper body. Their primary function is to pull the upper arm backward and downward. Your lats are particularly important in pulling down a rebound. In addition, developing your lats is necessary to provide muscular balance between your back and chest areas.

Shoulders

Your shoulders are made up of 11 muscles of which the deltoids are the most important. Your "delts" are actually composed of 3 separate parts or heads. Your anterior deltoid is found on the front of your shoulder and is used when raising your upper arm forward; your middle deltoid is found on the side of your shoulder and is involved when your upper arm is lifted sideways (away from your body.) Your posterior deltoid resides on the back of your shoulder and draws your upper arm backward. Several other deep muscles of your shoulder are sometimes referred to as the "internal rotators" (the subscapularis and teres major) and the "external rotators" (the infraspinatus and teres minor). In addition to performing rotation, these muscles also prevent shoulder impingement. Finally, the trapezius is often considered a part of the shoulder musculature. The trapezius is a kite-shaped muscle that covers the uppermost region of your back and the posterior section of your neck. The primary functions of your "traps" are to elevate your shoulders (as in shrugging), to adduct your scapulae (pinch your shoulder blades together) and to extend your head backward. Along with the muscles of your pectoral region, strong shoulders are a vital part of such skills as shooting, rebounding and passing.

ARMS

Biceps

The biceps brachii is the prominent muscle on the front part of your upper arm. It causes your arm to flex (or bend) at your elbow. As the name suggests, your biceps has 2 separate heads. In fact, the separation can sometimes be seen as a groove on a well-developed arm when the biceps are fully flexed. Your biceps assist your upper torso muscles – especially your lats – in pulling down a rebound.

Triceps

The triceps brachii is a horseshoe-shaped muscle located on the back of your upper arm. This muscle has 3 distinct heads – the long, lateral, and medial. The primary function of your triceps is to extend (or straighten) your arm at the elbow. Your triceps are utilized in many basketball skills, especially dribbling, passing and shooting.

Forearms

As stated earlier, your forearms are made up of 19 different muscles. These muscles may be divided into 2 groups on the basis of their position and functions. Your anterior group on the front part of your forearm causes flexion and pronation (turning your palm downward); your posterior group on the back part of your forearm causes extension and supination (turning your palm upward). Your forearms effect your wrists and hands which are important in skills such as shooting and dribbling.

ABDOMINALS

Rectus Abdominis

This long, narrow muscle extends vertically across the front of your abdomen from the lower rim of your rib cage to your pelvis. Its main function is to pull your torso toward your lower body. The fibers of this muscle are interrupted along their course by 3 horizontal fibrous bands, which give rise to the phrase "washboard abs" when describing an especially well-developed abdomen. The rectus abdominis is used during forced expiration and helps to control your breathing when you shoot free throws.

Obliques

Your external and internal obliques lie on both sides of your waist. The external oblique is a broad muscle whose fibers form a "V" across the front of your abdominal area, extending diagonally downward from your lower ribs to your pubic bone. The main function of this muscle is to bend your upper torso to the same side and to rotate your torso to the opposite side. Your internal obliques lie immediately under your external obliques on both sides of your abdomen. The fibers of the internal obliques form an inverted "V" along the front of your abdominal wall, extending diagonally upward from your pubic bone to your ribs. The internal obliques bend your upper body to the same side and turn your torso to the same side. Your obliques are used in skills in which you twist your torso such as a reverse or spin dribble.

Transverse Abdominis

This is the innermost layer of your abdominal musculature. Its fibers run horizontally across your abdomen. The primary function of this muscle is to constrict your abdomen. This muscle is also involved in forced expiration and control of your breathing.

LOWER BACK

Erector Spinae

The "spinal erectors" make up the main muscle group in your lower back. Their primary purpose is to extend (or straighten) the upper torso from a bent over position. Your low back muscles are used isometrically whenever you bend over at the waist and maintain a good defensive stance.

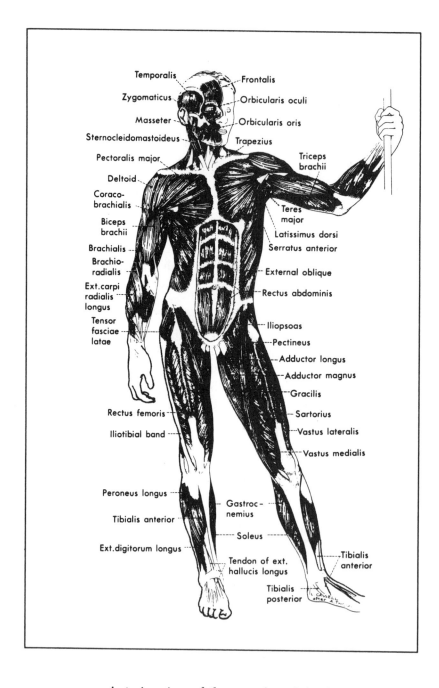

Anterior view of the muscles of the body

(From Human Anatomy and Physiology by B.G. King and M.J. Showers, 6th edition, Philadelphia: W.B. Saunders Company, 1969.)

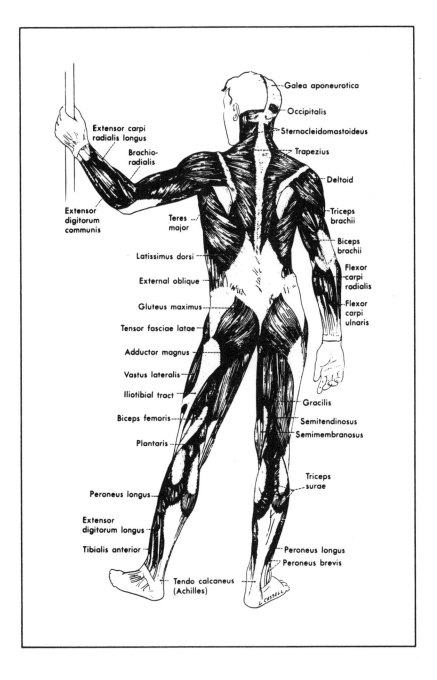

Posterior view of the muscles of the body

(From Human Anatomy and Physiology *by B.G. King and M.J. Showers, 6th edition, Philadelphia: W.B. Saunders Company, 1969.)*

2 THE "TEN COMMANDMENTS" OF STRENGTH TRAINING

The importance of strength, power, speed, conditioning, flexibility, agility and coordination is quite evident in the sport of basketball. Preparation for competition, therefore, should include strength training exercises, conditioning activities, stretching movements and the practicing of proper basketball technique for thousands and thousands of task-specific repetitions.

Remember that you are a basketball player – not a competitive weightlifter or a bodybuilder. There's nothing wrong with wanting to look better but don't forget that you could look like Tarzan and still play like Cheetah! Also keep in mind that attempting to see how much weight you can lift for 1 repetition is potentially dangerous and really doesn't prove anything anyway. In addition, multiple sets are extremely inefficient in terms of time and can significantly increase your risk of incurring an overuse injury – such as tendinitis – due to repetitive muscular trauma. Besides, a basketball game has never been decided by a bench press contest or a posedown!

The main purpose of a strength training program for basketball is to decrease your injury potential and its second purpose is to increase your performance potential. Make no mistake about it – strength training is primarily a mechanism to prevent injury. According to data collected for the NCAA Injury Surveillance System, the top 3 bodyparts injured during the 1991-92 men's college basketball season were the ankle (30%), the knee (12%) and the lower back (6%); the top 3 bodyparts injured in women's basketball were the ankle (27%), the knee (18%) and the lower leg (6%).Increasing the strength of your muscles, bones and connective tissue will reduce the likelihood that you will incur an injury while playing. That doesn't mean that you'll never get hurt ... sometimes injuries are a matter of being in the wrong spot at the wrong time. However, strength training will reduce your risk considerably. And, improving your functional strength will be an important step toward realizing your potential as a basketball player. A stronger muscle can produce more force; if you can produce more force, you'll require less effort and be able to perform your skills more quickly and more efficiently. Remember, strength training doesn't guarantee that you'll be a better player – you'll still have to practice your basketball skills in a correct manner so that you'll be more proficient in applying that force. Nevertheless, strength training will enhance your potential to become as good a basketball player as you possibly can.

The main purpose of a strength training program for basketball is to decrease your injury potential, and its second purpose is to increase your performance potential.

STRENGTH TRAINING PRINCIPLES

A safe, efficient, productive, comprehensive and physically demanding strength workout can be performed with virtually any type of equipment by using the following "Ten Commandants."

1. Train with a high level of intensity.

Intensity can be defined as "a percentage of momentary ability." In other words, intensity relates to the degree of the "inroads" – or amount of fatigue – you've made into your muscle at any given instant. When your muscles are fresh at the beginning of an exercise, your percentage of momentary ability is high, and your intensity (or effort) is obviously low. When your muscles are fatigued at the end of an exercise, your percentage of momentary ability is low, but now your intensity is high.

Research suggests that your level of intensity is the most important factor in determining your results from strength training – the harder that you train, the better your response. In the weight room, a high level of intensity is characterized by performing each exercise to the point of concentric muscular failure: when you've exhausted your muscles to the extent that you literally cannot raise the weight for any more repetitions. Failure to reach a desirable level of intensity – or muscular fatigue – will result in little or no strength gains. Evidence for this "threshold" is suggested by the "Overload Principle." Essentially, this principle states that in order to increase muscular size and strength, a muscle must be stressed – or "overloaded" – with a workload that is beyond its present capacity. Your intensity of effort must be great enough to exceed this threshold level so that a sufficient amount of muscular fatigue is produced. Given proper nourishment and an adequate amount of recovery between workouts, a muscle will adapt to these demands by increasing in size and strength. The extent to which this occurs then becomes a function of your inherited characteristics (i.e. muscle length, predominant muscle fiber type, etc.).

After reaching concentric muscular failure, you can increase the intensity even further by performing 3 to 5 additional post-fatigue repetitions. These post-fatigue reps may be either negatives or breakdowns and will allow you to overload your muscles in a safe, efficient manner.

Negatives (also called "forced reps") are accomplished by having a training partner raise the weight while the lifter resists the movement during the lowering (or "eccentric") phase. For example, suppose that you reached concentric muscular failure on a barbell bench press. Your partner would help you raise the weight off your chest until your arms are extended. Then, you lower the weight under control back to your chest. Your partner can even add a little extra resistance by pushing down on the bar as you lower it. In effect, these post-fatigue reps are positive-assisted and negative-resisted. (Raising the weight is sometimes referred to as the positive phase of a movement and involves a concentric muscular contraction; lowering the weight is typically referred to as the negative phase of a movement and involves an eccentric muscular contraction.) Performing a few negative repetitions at the end of an exercise will allow you to reach eccentric muscular failure – when your muscles have fatigued to the point that you can't even lower the weight! And that's why a set-to-failure followed immediately by several "negatives" is so brutally effective: you've managed to exhaust the muscle completely – both concentrically and eccentrically.

Regressions (also called "breakdowns" or "burnouts") are another way of achieving a greater level of intensity and concomitant muscular overload. When performing regressions, you (or your training partner) quickly reduce the starting weight by about 25 to 30 percent and the lifter does 3 to 5 post-fatigue reps with the lighter resistance. Let's say you did 14 reps with 100 pounds on the leg extension before reaching concentric muscular failure. You (or your partner) would immediately reduce the weight to about 70 to 75 pounds and would then attempt to perform 3 to 5 reps with the lighter weight .

In a certain sense these post-fatigue reps (either negatives or regressions) are a second set ... but they've come immediately after reaching muscular failure. Since there is little or no recovery time between these "sets," the additional post-fatigue reps are simply an extension of the first set.

It is also important to understand that an inverse relationship exists between time and intensity: as the time or length of an activity increases, your level of intensity decreases. Stated otherwise, you cannot train at a high level of intensity for long periods of time.

For example, suppose you had to sprint as fast as you possibly could for as long as you could. If you're like most people, you'd be able to run about 440 yards at an absolute breakneck speed before stopping due to total exhaustion. Your level of effort was extremely high but your time of activity was quite low. On the other hand, imagine that you were to run that same distance in 3 minutes. In this case, your level of intensity was rather low and your duration of activity was high.

The fact is that you can exercise for a short period of time with a high level of intensity or a long period of time with a low level of intensity. However, you cannot possibly train at a high level of intensity for a long period of time. In order to train at a reasonably high level of intensity, you must train for a relatively brief period of time.

The fact that your results are directly related to your level of effort shouldn't be much of a surprise. It's like anything else in life: how hard you work at your studies, your practices, your job and even your relationships will largely determine your success at those endeavors. This also applies to your strength training.

Negatives, or "forced reps," are accomplished by having a training partner raise the weight while the lifter resists the movement during the lowering, or "eccentric," phase.

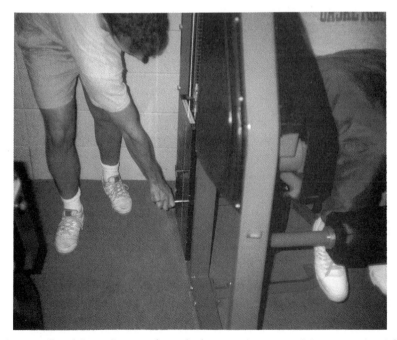

Regressions, or "breakdowns," are performed when you (or your training partner) quickly reduce the starting weight by 25 to 30 percent and the lifter does 3-5 post-fatigue reps with the lighter resistance.

Indeed, a high level of intensity is an absolute requirement for optimal gains in muscular size and strength.

2. Attempt to increase the resistance used or the repetitions performed every workout.

Suppose that today you did a set of leg curls for 10 reps with 100 pounds and a month later you're still doing 10 reps with 100 pounds. It's not likely that you've gotten any stronger. On the other hand, what if you were able to do 11 reps with 120 pounds a month later? In this case, you were able to perform 10 percent more reps with 20 percent more weight. That's excellent progress over a period of 1 month!

The fact of the matter is that for a muscle to increase in size and strength, it must be forced to do progressively harder work. Once again, the Overload Principle is being applied. Your muscles must be overloaded with a workload that is increased steadily and systematically throughout the course of your program. This is often referred to as "progressive overload." Legend has it that Milo of Croton, an Olympic athlete in ancient Greece, periodically lifted a baby bull on his shoulders. Milo's strength increased as the bull increased in size and weight. Indeed, this crude method of progression was responsible for Milo's strength gains. (No bull!)

Therefore, every time you work out you should attempt to increase either the weight you use or the repetitions you perform in relation to your previous workout. This can be viewed as a "double progressive" technique (resistance and repetitions). Challenging your muscles in this manner will force them to adapt to the imposed demands (or stress).

Each time you attain the maximum number of repetitions, you should increase the resistance for your next workout. Your progressions need not be in Herculean leaps and bounds, but the weight must always be challenging. The resistance should be increased in an amount that you are comfortable with. Fortunately, this may be accomplished much more systematically than the method used by Milo and his growing bull! Your muscles will respond better if the progressions in resistance are 5 percent or less. But again, remember that the resistance must always be challenging.

You shouldn't really be concerned with what you can lift relative to another player. However, you should be concerned with what you can lift relative to your previous performances. In other words, don't compare your strength to anyone else – just make sure that you are as strong as you can be!

3. Perform 1 to 3 sets of each exercise.

If performed properly, traditional multiple set routines (i.e. more than 1 set) can be effective in "overloading" a muscle. They've been used successfully by competitive weightlifters and bodybuilders for decades. And, since many strength coaches have competed in weightlifting meets and bodybuilding events, it's no surprise that most high schools, colleges and professional teams incorporate a traditional multiple set program.

Few strength and fitness professionals ever recommend performing more than 3 sets per exercise. Anything more than about 3 sets is generally considered to be an unproductive form of manual labor. The question is: Can performing 1 set of each exercise in a high intensity fashion give you the same results as performing 2 or 3 sets? Absolutely. Remember, in order for a muscle to increase in size and strength it must be fatigued or overloaded. It's that simple. It really doesn't matter whether you fatigue your muscles in 1 set or several sets – as long as your muscles experience a certain level of exhaustion. When performing multiple sets, the cumulative effect of each successive set makes deeper inroads into your muscle thereby creating muscular fatigue; when performing a single-set-to-failure, the cumulative effect of each successive repetition makes deeper inroads into your muscle thereby creating muscular fatigue. In fact, numerous research studies have shown that there are no significant differences when performing either 1, 2 or 3 sets of an exercise, provided, of course, that 1 set is done with an appropriate level of intensity (i.e. to the point of concentric muscular failure). Following concentric muscular failure, you can further overload your muscles by incorporating a few post-fatigue reps – either negatives or regressions.

Both a single-set-to-failure and multiple sets produce muscular fatigue. However, multiple sets do not necessarily guarantee that your muscles received a sufficient level of muscular fatigue. Indeed, a large amount of low-intensity exercise will do very little in the way of increasing strength. But, performing 1 set of an exercise to the point where you cannot do any more repetitions always achieves a desirable level of muscular exhaustion.

How does this happen in only 1 set? Well, suppose that you are to perform a set of leg extensions with 100 pounds. In order to overcome inertia and give movement to the 100 pounds of resistance, your quadriceps must exert slightly more than 100 pounds of force. The weight will not move if a force less than or equal to 100 pounds is applied. During the first repetition, your intensity is low. At this point, only a small percentage of your available muscle fibers is being used – just enough to move the weight. As you perform each repetition, your intensity increases progressively and you're making deeper inroads into your muscle. Some of your muscle fibers will fatigue and will no longer be able to keep up with the increasing metabolic demands. Fresh fibers are simultaneously recruited to assist the fatigued fibers in generating ample force. This process continues until the last repetition when concentric muscular failure is finally reached and your intensity is the highest. Now, your remaining fibers cannot collectively produce enough force to raise the weight. During this final repetition, the cumulative effect of each preceding repetition has fatigued the muscle thereby providing a sufficient – and efficient – stimulus for muscular growth. One set of each exercise can indeed produce striking results, but each set must be done with a maximal effort. Your muscles should be completely fatigued at the end of each exercise.

It should be noted that your first few reps are the least productive because your intensity is low. On the other hand, your very last rep is the most productive because your intensity is very high.

Everything you do in the weight room should have a purpose. That purpose is to reduce your risk of injury and to realize your potential as a basketball player. You should emphasize the quality of work done in the weight room rather than the quantity of work. Don't do meaningless sets in the weight room – make every single exercise count. Remember, the most efficient program is one that produces the maximum possible results in the least amount of time. After all, why perform several sets when you can obtain similar results from 2 sets, or even 1 set in a fraction of the time?

Truly, 1 set done with a maximal level of effort is the metabolic equivalent of several sets done with a submaximal level of effort. As such, multiple sets are relatively inefficient in terms of time and, therefore, are undesirable. Performing too many sets – or too many exercises – can also create a catabolic training effect that retards muscular growth. When this happens, your muscles are broken down in such an extreme manner that your body is unable to regenerate muscle tissue. This results in a loss of size and strength. Also keep in mind that performing too many sets increases your risk of an overuse injury.

Don't be misled by the brevity or simplicity of a program that calls for 1 set of each exercise done with a high level of intensity. An exercise performed with a high level of intensity can be very productive and effective. In fact, University of Toledo Strength Coach Ken Mannie has stated that high intensity strength training is "the most productive, most efficient and without a doubt, the most demanding form of strength training known to man." When you perform an exercise to the point of muscular failure and follow it by a few negative or regressive repetitions, you'll quickly realize why it's called "high intensity!" Don't forget, a submaximal effort will yield submaximal results.

4. Reach concentric muscular failure within a prescribed number of repetitions.

In general, you should reach concentric muscular failure within 10-15 reps for exercises involving your hips, 8-12 reps for your legs and midsection and 6-10 reps for your upper torso. However, some movements have rather short ranges of motion and require a minor adjustment in the minimum number of reps to ensure that your muscles are under tension for an adequate amount of time. Generally, these are single-joint movements that have a range of motion of about 90 degrees or less. Therefore, shoulder shrugs and internal/external rotation along with exercises for your forearms should be done for 8 to 12 reps to guarantee a desirable amount of contraction time.

If concentric muscular failure occurs before you reach the lower level of the repetition range, the weight is too heavy and should be reduced for your next workout. If the upper level of the repetition range is exceeded before you experience muscular exhaustion, the weight is too light and should be increased for your next workout by 5 percent or less.

If you're just beginning an exercise program, or if you change the exercises in your routine, it may take several workouts before you find a challenging weight. That's okay – simply continue to make progressions in the resistance as needed.

It should be noted that attempting a 1-repetition maximum or performing low-repetition movements (i.e. less than about 3 or 4 reps) significantly increases your risk of injury. Likewise, once an activity exceeds the recommended number of reps, it becomes a test of endurance rather than strength.

5. Perform each repetition with proper technique.

A quality program begins with a quality repetition. Indeed, the repetition is the most basic and integral aspect of a strength program. A repetition consists of raising the weight to the mid-range position, pausing briefly and then returning the weight to the starting/stretched position.

A quality rep is performed by raising and lowering the weight in a deliberate, controlled manner. Lifting a weight in a rapid, explosive fashion is ill-advised for 2 reasons: (1) it exposes your muscles, joint structures and connective tissue to potentially dangerous forces which magnify the likelihood of an injury while strength training and (2) it introduces momentum into the movement which makes the exercise less productive and less efficient. Lifting a weight in about 1 to 2 seconds will guarantee that you're exercising in a safe, efficient manner.

It should take about 3 to 4 seconds to lower the weight back to the starting/stretched position. It stands to reason that the lowering portion of the movement should be emphasized for a longer time because you can lower more weight than you can raise. In fact, some research suggests that a fresh muscle can lower approximately 40 percent more than it can raise. So, if you can lift 100 pounds, you can lower about 140 pounds. The lowering of the weight should also be emphasized because it makes the exercise more efficient: the same muscles that are used to raise the weight concentrically are also used to lower it eccentrically. The only difference is that when you raise a weight, your muscles are shortening against tension, and when you lower a weight, your muscles are lengthening against tension. So, by emphasizing the lowering of a weight, each repetition becomes more efficient and each set becomes more productive. Because a muscle under tension lengthens as you lower it, lowering the weight in a controlled manner also ensures that the exercised muscle is being stretched properly and safely.

In effect, each repetition should be roughly 4 to 6 seconds in length. Most strength coaches who are opposed to explosive, ballistic movements in the weight room consider a 4 to 6 second rep as a general guideline for lifting "under control" or "without momentum."

Finally, a quality rep is done throughout the greatest possible range of motion that safety allows – from a position of full stretch to a position of full muscular contraction and back to a position of full stretch. Exercising throughout a full range of motion will allow you to maintain (or perhaps increase) your flexibility, which reduces your potential for injury. Furthermore, it ensures that you are exercising your entire muscle – not just a portion of it – thereby making the movement more efficient. Indeed, studies have shown that full-range exercise is necessary for a full-range effect. This does not imply that you should avoid limited range movements altogether. During rehabilitation, for example, you can exercise throughout a pain-free range and still manage to stimulate some gains in strength. However, full range movements are more productive and should be performed whenever possible.

Remember, how you lift a weight is more important than how much weight you lift. Your strength training will be safer and more efficient by performing each rep with proper technique.

6. Strength train for no more than 1 hour per workout.

More may be better when it comes to assists, rebounds and points scored, but more isn't necessarily better when it comes to strength training. Recall that if you are training with a high level of intensity, you literally cannot exercise for a long period of time.

The duration of your workout depends on several factors, such as the size of the facility, the amount of equipment, the preparation for each exercise (changing plates, moving pins, etc.), the number of people in the facility, the transition time between each set, the availability of supervisory personnel and the managerial ability of those personnel. Generally speaking, however, you should be able to complete a productive workout in less than 1 hour. Under normal circumstances, if you are spending much more than an hour in the weight room then you are probably not training with a desirable level of intensity.

The transition time between each exercise will vary with your level of conditioning. You should proceed from 1 exercise to the next as soon as you "catch your breath" or feel that you can produce a maximal level of effort. After an initial period of adjustment, you should be able to recover adequately within 1 to 3 minutes. Training with a minimal amount of recovery time between exercises will elicit a metabolic conditioning effect that cannot be approached by traditional multiple set programs. Anyone who has been through a rigorous high intensity training session knows exactly what this means. Indeed, the effects of such workouts must be experienced to be fully appreciated!

7. Perform no more than about 15 exercises each workout.

A comprehensive strength training program for basketball consists of about 15 exercises during each workout. The focal point for most of these exercises should be your major muscle groups (i.e. your hips, legs and upper torso). Include 1 exercise for your hips, hamstrings, quadriceps, calves/dorsi flexors, biceps, triceps, forearms, abdominals and lower back. Because your shoulder joint allows movement at many different angles, 2 exercises should be selected for your chest, back (your "lats") and shoulders. You should select any exercises that you prefer in order to train those bodyparts.

Occasionally, you may wish to perform an additional movement to emphasize a particular bodypart. That's all right, as long as your strength gains continue. If you start to level off or "plateau" in an exercise, it's probably due to a catabolic effect from doing too many exercises.

8. Whenever possible, work your muscles from largest to smallest.

Exercise your hips first, then go to your legs (hams, quads and calves or dorsi flexors), upper torso (chest, back and shoulders), arms (biceps, triceps and forearms), abs and finally your lower back.

It is especially important not to exercise your arms before exercising your upper torso. Multiple joint (or compound) movements done for your upper body require the use of your arms to assist the movement. Your arms are the "weak link" in the exercise because they are smaller. So, if you fatigue your arms first, you will weaken an already weak link, thereby limiting the workload placed on the muscles of your upper torso. Likewise, your legs are the weak link when performing exercises for your hips and buttocks. Therefore, avoid training your legs – especially your hams and quads – before performing an exercise for your hips, like the leg press.

9. Strength train 2 to 3 times per week on nonconsecutive days.

Intense strength training places great demands and stress on your muscles. Your muscles must receive an adequate amount of recovery between strength workouts in order to adapt to those demands.

Believe it or not, your muscles do not get stronger while you work out – your muscles get stronger while you recover from your workout. When you lift weights, your muscle tissue is broken down, and the recovery process allows your muscle time to rebuild itself. Think of this as allowing a wound to heal. If you had a scab and picked at it every day, you would delay the healing process, but if you left it alone you would permit the damaged tissue time to heal. There may be some individual variations in recovery ability. However, a period of about 48-72 hours is necessary for muscle tissue to recover sufficiently from a strength workout. A period of at least 48 hours is also required to replenish your depleted carbohydrate stores. Therefore, it is suggested that you lift 2 to 3 times per week on nonconsecutive days (e.g. Monday, Wednesday and Friday). Performing any more than 3 sessions a week can gradually become counterproductive due to a catabolic effect. This occurs when the demands you have placed on your muscles have exceeded your recovery ability.

Some research has indicated that a muscle will begin to progressively lose size and strength if it isn't exercised within about 96 hours of it's previous workout. That's why it's important to continue strength training even while in-season or while competing. However, you will need to reduce your workouts to twice a week due to the increased activity level of practices and games. One session should be done as soon as possible following your game and another no later than 48 hours before your next game. So, if you play on Saturdays and Tuesdays, you should strength train on Sundays and Wednesdays (or Thursdays – providing that it's not within 48 hours of your next game). From time to time, you may only be able to strength train once a week because of a particularly heavy schedule (e.g. playing 3 games in 1 week, participating in a holiday or post-season tournament, etc.)

How do you know if you've had sufficient recovery time? You should see a gradual improvement in the amount of weight and/or the number of repetitions that you're able to do over the course of several weeks. If not, then you're probably not getting enough of a recovery between workouts. Remember, if you want a muscle to get larger and stronger you must stress it and rest it!

10. Keep accurate records of your performance.

The importance of accurate record keeping cannot be overemphasized. Records are a log of what you've accomplished during each and every exercise of each and every strength session. In a sense, a workout card is a history of your activities in the weight room.

A workout card can be an extremely valuable tool to monitor progress and make your workouts more meaningful. It can also be used to identify exercises in which a plateau has been reached. In the unfortunate event of an injury, you can also gauge the effectiveness of the rehabilitative process if there is a record of your pre-injury strength levels.

A workout card can take an infinite number of appearances. However, you should be able to record your bodyweight, the date of each workout, the weight used for each exercise, the number of repetitions performed for each exercise, the order in which the exercises were completed and any necessary seat adjustments.

In addition, it's helpful to separate the exercises according to bodyparts along with the suggested number of exercises that are to be performed for each bodypart. The card can list specific exercises and the more common movements (e.g. leg curl, leg extension, bench press) and/or may contain blank spaces so that you can fill in your own menu of exercises. The recommended repetition ranges should also be given for each exercise along with spaces to record your seat adjustments. A sample workout card is shown in on the following page.

The area to the immediate right of this information is where you can record the data from your strength sessions. The chart below details how to record the weight used, the repetitions performed and the order in which you completed the exercises.

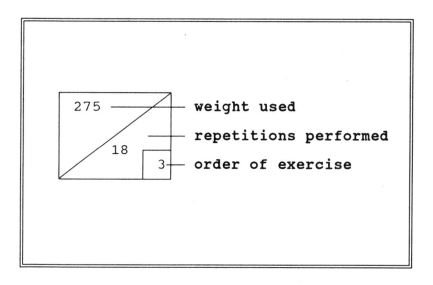

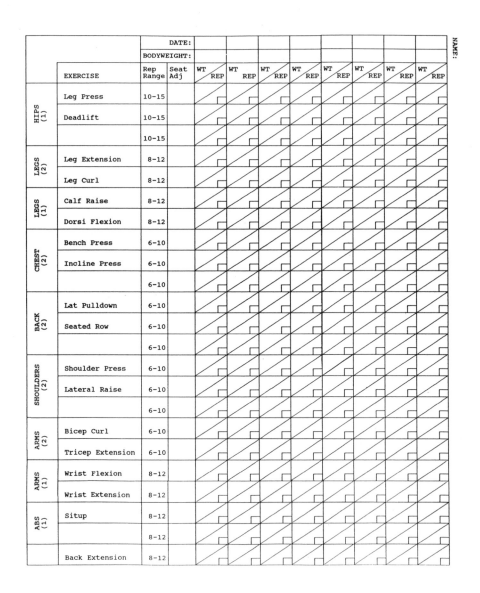

Sample Workout Card

3 WEIGHT TRAINING EXERCISES AND THEIR DESCRIPTIONS

There are literally scores of fitness manufacturers who produce thousands of pieces of exercise equipment. This chapter will highlight several types of the most respected, productive and prevalent types of equipment modalities that are available for use – barbells, dumbbells, Nautilus, Universal, plate-loading and manual resistance – along with 2 of the more recent innovative devices – the Gravitron and trap bar.

Barbells and dumbbells (i.e. "free weights") are extremely popular pieces of equipment that have been used by virtually every weight trainee at one time or another. Most high schools, universities, YMCAs and commercial fitness centers equip their weight rooms with at least some barbells and dumbbells.

When Nautilus arrived on the fitness scene in 1970, it revolutionized the way people thought about exercise. Over the years, the name "Nautilus" has become synonymous with fitness and exercise. Today, Nautilus continues to be the most recognized name in fitness, a leader in education and remains perhaps the most popular equipment-of-choice among fitness enthusiasts.

Universal equipment – with its single stations and Multi-Gyms – is quite versatile and has gained widespread acceptance as a training modality, especially at high schools, universities and YMCAs.

Various plate-loading machines are produced by many companies and are growing quickly in terms of being popular, effective and cost-efficient tools-of-the-trade.

Manual resistance (MR) is often referred to as a "productive alternative" for developing strength when equipment isn't available. It is an extremely effective way of strength training in which a partner supplies the resistance.

Finally, the Gravitron is a machine that basically gives the user mechanical assistance in performing dips and chins; the trap bar is a productive tool that can be used to perform several exercises in a manner that is safer and more effective than a barbell.

The following pages will describe and illustrate 32 of the most widely-used and most productive exercises that can be performed using the previously-mentioned equipment. Included in the descriptions are the muscle(s) used in each exercise (if more than one muscle is involved, the first muscle listed is the prime mover), the suggested repetition range, the type of movement and notes on making the exercises safer and more productive.

DEADLIFT

Trap Bar

Dumbbell

Muscles used: hips, hamstrings, quadriceps, lower back

Suggested reps: 10-15

Type of movement: multiple joint

Notes:

- Use an alternating grip (dominant palm forward, nondominant palm backward) with a barbell; use a parallel grip (palms facing each other) with dumbbells and the trap bar.
- Your feet should be placed slightly wider than shoulder width apart. Most of your weight should be centered on your heels, not on your toes. Keep your arms straight, your head up and your back flat throughout this exercise.
- Don't bounce the weight off the floor between reps.
- You can use wrist straps if you have difficulty maintaining your grip.
- Deadlifts may be inadvisable if you have low back pain or an exceptionally long torso and/or legs.
- Avoid lifting your hips up too early during the execution of this movement. Raising your hips up too early negates their effectiveness and causes you to perform the movement entirely with your lower back. Ideally, your hips, legs and lower back should work together, but most of the work should be done by your hips and legs.
- Don't lock your knees in the mid-range of a repetition. This takes the tension off your muscles and may hyperextend your knees.
- When you lower the weight, don't go beyond a point where your upper legs are parallel to the ground.

LEG PRESS

Universal

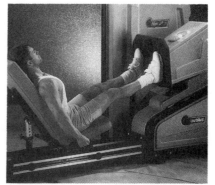

Nautilus

Plate-loading

Muscles used: hips, hamstrings, quadriceps

Suggested reps: 10-15

Type of movement: multiple joint

Notes:

- Adjust the seat so that the angle between your upper and lower legs is about 90 degrees in the starting position. If this isn't possible because of your leg length, have your partner help you lift the movement arm forward a little bit. Thereafter, during each rep, don't go beyond a point where the angle between your upper and lower legs is less than 90 degrees.
- Your feet should be placed slightly wider than shoulder width apart. If possible, position your lower legs perpendicular to the base of the foot pedal(s).

- Use the upper foot pedals on the Universal station whenever possible. The lower foot pedals tend to create excessive shear forces in the knee joint.
- Push through your heels, not through the balls of your feet.
- Avoid locking or "snapping" your legs in the mid-range of a repetition. This takes the tension off your muscles and may hyperextend your knees.

HIP ABDUCTION

Nautilus

Universal

Manual Resistance

Muscles used: hip abductors (gluteus medius)

Suggested reps: 8-12

Type of movement: single joint

Notes:

- Spread your legs apart as far as possible (or lift your leg as high as possible) during the mid-range of each repetition.
- Lower your leg(s) back to the starting position (legs together) at the end of every rep to obtain a proper stretch.
- Avoid bending your body forward as you perform this exercise.

HIP ADDUCTION

Nautilus

Universal   **Manual Resistance**

Muscles used: hip adductors (inner thigh)

Suggested reps: 8-12

Type of movement: single joint

Notes:

- Bring your legs completely together (or bring one leg to the other) during the mid-range of each repetition.
- Return your leg(s) back to the starting position (legs apart) at the completion of each rep to ensure a proper stretch.

LEG CURL

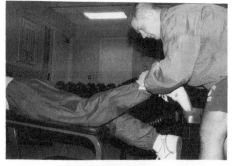

Manual Resistance

Universal

Muscles used: hamstrings

Suggested reps: 8-12

Type of movement: single joint

Notes:

- The top of your kneecaps should be positioned just over the edge of the pad, not on the pad.
- Pull your heel(s) as close to your buttocks as possible in the mid-range of each repetition. The angle between your upper and lower leg(s) should be about 90 degrees or less. (This could be deceiving if the machine's pad is "humped" or angled rather than flat.)
- It's okay to raise your hips as you do this movement because this action actually increases your range of motion.

- Lower the resistance back to the starting position (legs straight) at the end of each rep to provide a proper stretch.
- This movement may be done unilaterally (one side at a time) if you have a knee injury, a gross strength imbalance or desire a training variation.
- Leg curls may be inadvisable if you have low back pain.

LEG EXTENSION

Manual Resistance

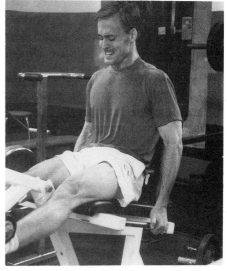

Plate-loading

Muscles used: quadriceps

Suggested reps: 8-12

Type of movement: single joint

Notes:

- When performing this movement on a machine, there should be little or no space between the backs of your knees and the front edge of the seat pad; likewise, there should be little or no space between your buttocks and the back pad.
- Extend your lower leg(s) up as high as possible during the mid-range of each repetition.

- Lower the weight all the way back to the starting position at the completion of every rep to obtain a proper stretch.
- This movement may be done unilaterally if you have a knee injury, a gross strength imbalance or desire a training variation.

CALF RAISE

Nautilus

Plate-loading

Muscles used: calves

Suggested reps: 8-12

Type of movement: single joint

Notes:

- Rise up on your toes as high as possible during the mid-range of each repetition.
- Lower yourself all the way back to the starting position at the end of each rep to ensure a proper stretch.
- Keep your legs straight while performing this exercise.
- This movement may be done unilaterally if you have an ankle injury, a gross strength imbalance or desire a training variation.

- Traditionally, this exercise is done with a weight placed on the shoulders – either a barbell or a machine's movement arm. However, this should be avoided because it involves spinal compression.
- Calf raises may be inadvisable if you have shin splints.

DORSI FLEXION

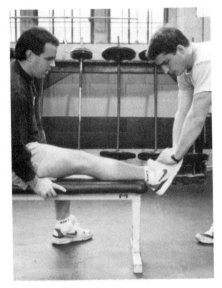

Manual Resistance

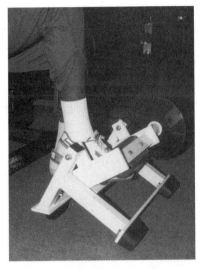

Plate-loading

Muscles used: dorsi flexors (tibialis anterior)

Suggested reps: 8-12

Type of movement: single joint

Notes:

- Pull your foot toward your lower leg as much as possible during the mid-range of each repetition.
- Extend your foot completely at the end of each rep to provide a proper stretch.

BENCH PRESS

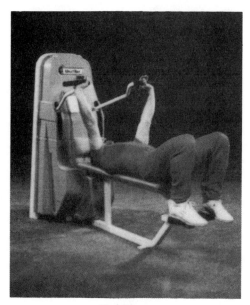

Nautilus

Dumbbell

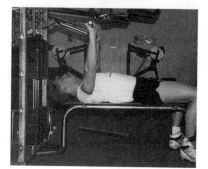

Universal

Muscles used: chest, anterior deltoid, triceps

Suggested reps: 6-10

Type of movement: multiple joint

Notes:

- Your hands should be placed slightly wider than shoulder width apart. An excessively wide grip will reduce the movement's range of motion.
- Lower the resistance all the way down to the middle portion of your chest during each rep; if you're using a barbell, don't allow the bar to bounce off your chest.
- Don't lock or "snap" your elbows in the mid-range of a repetition. This takes the tension off your muscles and may hyperextend your elbows.

- Keep your buttocks against the bench when performing this movement.
- Placing your feet on a stool will flatten your lumbar area against the bench, thereby reducing any stress in your lower back.

INCLINE PRESS

Dumbbell

Barbell

Muscles used: chest (upper), anterior deltoid, triceps

Suggested reps: 6-10

Type of movement: multiple joint

Notes:

- Your hands should be placed slightly wider than shoulder width apart. An excessively wide grip will reduce the movement's range of motion.
- Lower the resistance all the way down to the upper part of your chest during each rep; if you're using a barbell, don't allow the bar to bounce off your chest.
- Don't lock or "snap" your elbows in the mid-range of a repetition. This takes the tension off your muscles and may hyperextend your elbows.
- Keep your buttocks against the bench (or seat pad) as you perform this exercise.
- Placing your feet on a stool (or footrest) will flatten your lumbar area against the bench, thereby reducing any stress in your lower back.

DECLINE PRESS

Plate-loading

Dumbbell

Universal

Muscles used: chest (lower), anterior deltoid, triceps

Suggested reps: 6-10

Type of movement: multiple joint

Notes:

- Your hands should be placed slightly wider than shoulder width apart. An excessively wide grip will reduce the movement's range of motion.
- Lower the resistance all the way down (or back) to the lower portion of your chest during each rep; if you're using a barbell, don't allow the bar to bounce off your chest.
- Don't lock or "snap" your elbows in the mid-range of a repetition. This takes the tension off your muscles and may hyperextend your elbows.
- Keep your buttocks against the bench (or seat pad) when doing this exercise.

BENT ARM FLY

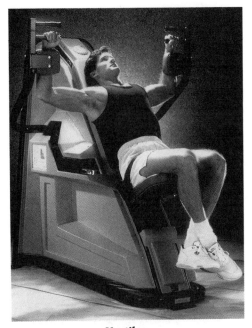

Nautilus

Dumbbell

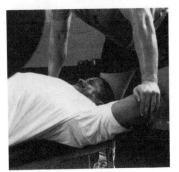

Manual Resistance

Muscles used: chest, anterior deltoid

Suggested reps: 6-10

Type of movement: single joint

Notes:

- If you're using a machine or manual resistance, bring your elbows as close together as possible during the mid-range of each repetition.
- If you're using dumbbells, try to maintain a 90 degree angle between your upper and lower arms as you raise and lower the weight. (Pretend that you're hugging a tree!) Extending your arms as you raise the dumbbells will turn the bent arm fly into a dumbbell bench press.
- Return your arms back to the starting position (arms apart) at the end of each rep to obtain a proper stretch.

- Keep your buttocks against the bench (or seat pad) when performing this exercise.
- Placing your feet on a stool will flatten your lumbar area against the bench, thereby reducing any stress in your lower back.
- Most machines allow you to do this movement unilaterally in the event that you have a shoulder injury, a strength imbalance or desire a training variation.

DIP

Nautilus

Universal

Muscles used: chest (lower), anterior deltoid, triceps

Suggested reps: 6-10

Type of movement: multiple joint

Notes:

- Don't lock or "snap" your elbows in the mid-range of a repetition. This takes the tension off your muscles and may hyperextend your elbows.
- If you are unable to do 6 reps in strict form with your bodyweight, you can do this movement on the Gravitron or a selectorized-plate-loading version (in the seated position). The Gravitron allows you to do dips with a percentage of your bodyweight by giving you mechanical assistance; most selectorized/plate-loading versions allow you to choose a resistance that is less than your bodyweight.

- Lower yourself back to the starting position (elbows bent about 90 degrees) at the end of every rep to ensure a proper stretch.
- Once you are able to do 10 reps in strict form with your bodyweight, you can increase the resistance by adding extra weight to your waist. Most selectorized/plate-loading versions also permit you to choose a resistance that is more than your bodyweight.

LAT PULLDOWN

Nautilus

Universal

Muscles used: back (lats), biceps, forearms
Suggested reps: 6-10
Type of movement: multiple joint
Notes:

- Your hands should be spaced approximately shoulder width apart with your palms up. Pull the bar (or handles) to the upper part of your chest and rotate your elbows backward during the mid-range of each repetition. Some handles permit you to use a parallel grip. You can also space your hands several inches wider than shoulder width apart with your palms down. In either case, pull the bar (or handles) behind your head and draw your elbows to your sides.
- Return the weight to the starting position (arms fully extended) at the end of each rep to provide a proper stretch.
- You can use wrist straps if you have difficulty maintaining your grip.
- Performing this movement with an overhand grip (palms down) is not as efficient as performing it with a parallel or an underhand grip (palms up). With an underhand grip, your forearm bones run parallel to one another; an overhand grip causes the bones to cross forming an "X." When this happens, your bicep tendon wraps around the bone, creating a biomechanical disadvantage.
- This exercise becomes a single joint movement (which does not involve your biceps or forearms) when using manual resistance because the resistance is applied above your elbows, instead of to your hands.
- Overhand lat pulldowns may be inadvisable if you have shoulder impingement.

SEATED ROW

Plate-loading

Universal

Manual Resistance

Muscles used: back (lats), biceps, forearms

Suggested reps: 6-10

Type of movement: multiple joint

Notes:

- Your grip can be palms up, palms down or parallel depending upon the machine's handles or bar. If you're using manual resistance or Universal equipment, pull the movement arm to your mid-section during the mid-range of every repetition; if you're using a Nautilus or plate-loading device, pull the movement arm to a point just below your shoulders.
- Lower the resistance back to the starting position (arms fully extended) at the end of each rep to ensure a proper stretch.

- It's okay to lean back slightly during this exercise. However, keep your upper torso in the same position throughout the movement. Don't bend back and forth at the waist as you raise and lower the resistance – movement should only occur around your shoulder and elbow.
- You can use wrist straps if you have difficulty maintaining your grip.
- Performing this movement with an overhand grip (palms down) is not as efficient as performing it with a parallel or an underhand grip (palms up) for the same reason as described under "Lat Pulldown."

BENT OVER ROW

Manual Resistance

Dumbbell

Muscles used: back (lats), biceps, forearms

Suggested reps: 6-10

Type of movement: multiple joint

Notes:

- If you're using a dumbbell, place one hand and one knee on a bench. Pull the weight up to your shoulder in the mid-range of each repetition. If you're using manual resistance, lie prone on a bench with your shoulders slightly over the edge. Keeping your upper arms perpendicular to your torso, lift your elbows upward as high as possible.
- If you're using a dumbbell, lower the resistance back to the starting position (arm fully extended) at the end of each rep to ensure a proper stretch; if you're using manual resistance, try to maintain a 90 degree angle between your upper and lower arms as you perform the movement.
- It's natural for your shoulder to change its position as you perform this exercise. However, the movement of your shoulder should not be excessive or used to throw the weight – movement should only occur around your shoulder and elbow.
- You can use wrist straps if you have difficulty maintaining your grip.
- This exercise becomes a single joint movement (which does not involve your biceps or forearms) when using manual resistance because the resistance is applied above your elbows, instead of to your hands.

PULLOVER

Nautilus

Plate-loading

Muscles used: back (lats)

Suggested reps: 6-10

Type of movement: single joint

Notes:

- If you're using a machine, pull the movement arm to your mid-section during the mid-range of every repetition. Keep your palms open and your fingers extended so that you exert force against the movement arm with your elbows, not your hands. If you're using a dumbbell, lie supine on a bench and pull the weight to a position over your chest at arms length. Keep your arms straight throughout the dumbbell pullover.

- Lower the resistance back as far as possible to the starting position (elbows near or slightly past your head) to obtain a proper stretch.
- Pullovers may be inadvisable if you have low back pain or shoulder impingement.

CHIN

Universal

Nautilus

Muscles used: back (lats), biceps, forearms
Suggested reps: 6-10
Type of movement: multiple joint
Notes:

- Your hands should be spaced approximately shoulder width apart with your palms up. Pull yourself up so that your upper chest touches the bar and your elbows are rotated backward during the mid-range of each repetition. You can also space your hands several inches wider than shoulder width apart with your palms down. In this case, you can either pull yourself up so that the bar touches either your upper chest or behind your head and your elbows are drawn to your sides. (This is typically referred to as a "pullup.")
- Lower yourself back to the starting position (arms fully extended) at the end of each rep to provide a proper stretch.
- You can use wrist straps if you have difficulty maintaining your grip.

- Performing this movement with an overhand grip (palms down) is not as efficient as using an underhand grip (palms up) for the same reason as described under "Lat Pulldown."
- If you are unable to do 6 reps in strict form with your bodyweight, you can do this exercise on the Gravitron or perform lat pulldowns. The Gravitron allows you to do a chin/ pullup movement with a percentage of your bodyweight by giving you mechanical assistance.
- Once you are able to do 10 reps in strict form with your bodyweight, you can increase the resistance by adding extra weight to your waist.
- Pullups (palms down) may be inadvisable if you have shoulder impingement.

SHOULDER PRESS

Barbell

Nautilus

Muscles used: anterior deltoid, triceps

Suggested reps: 6-10

Type of movement: multiple joint

Notes:

- If you are using a machine with an adjustable seat, position it so that the tops of your shoulders are nearly touching the handles. If you are doing this exercise on Universal equipment, you should be seated facing away from the machine's weight stack.
- Your hands should be placed slightly wider than shoulder width apart. An excessively wide grip will reduce the movement's range of motion.
- Don't lock or "snap" your elbows in the mid-range of a repetition. This takes the tension off your muscles and may hyperextend your elbows.

- Lower the bar (or handles) all the way down to your shoulders during each rep to provide a proper stretch.
- Keep your buttocks against the seat pad and your torso against the back pad as you perform this exercise.
- Placing your feet on a stool (or footrest) will flatten your lumbar area against the back pad, thereby reducing any stress in your lower back.
- If you're using a barbell, you can lower the bar either behind your head or in front of it. However, lowering the bar behind your head may be inadvisable if you have shoulder impingement.

LATERAL RAISE

Dumbbell

Manual Resistance

Muscles used: middle deltoid

Suggested reps: 6-10

Type of movement: single joint

Notes:

- Keep your arms fairly straight and raise the resistance away from your sides until your arms are parallel to the floor. Don't lift your arms beyond this point.
- Your palms should be facing down in the mid-range position (arms parallel to the floor).
- Return to the starting position (arms at your sides) at the end of every rep to ensure a proper stretch.

- Avoid throwing the resistance by using your legs or by swinging your upper torso back and forth – movement should only occur around your shoulder.
- This movement may be done unilaterally if you have a shoulder injury, a gross strength imbalance or desire a training variation.

FRONT RAISE

Dumbbell

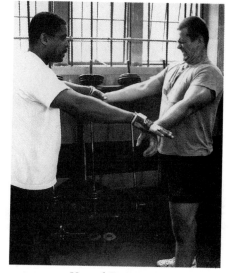

Manual Resistance

Muscles used: anterior deltoid

Suggested reps: 6-10

Type of movement: single joint

Notes:

- Keep your arms fairly straight and raise the resistance in front of you until your arms are parallel to the floor. Don't lift your arms beyond this point.
- Your palms should be facing each other in the mid-range position (arms parallel to the floor).
- Return to the starting position (arms at your sides) at the end of each rep to obtain a proper stretch.

- Avoid throwing the resistance by using your legs or by swinging your upper torso back and forth – movement should only occur around your shoulder.
- This exercise may be done unilaterally if you have a shoulder injury, a gross strength imbalance or desire a training variation.

BENT OVER RAISE

Manual Resistance

Plate-loading

Dumbbell

Muscles used: posterior deltoid, trapezius

Suggested reps: 6-10

Type of movement: single joint

Notes:

- If you're using Universal equipment, position yourself so that one side of your body faces the weight stack. Bend over at the waist and grasp the handle with the hand that is furthest away from the machine. If you're using any other equipment, lie prone on a bench with your shoulders slightly over the edge. Keeping your arm(s) straight and perpendicular to your torso, raise the weight upward as high as possible in the mid-range of each repetition.

- Lower the resistance back to the starting position (arm(s) hanging down) at the end of each rep to ensure a proper stretch.
- It's natural for your shoulder to change its position as you perform this exercise. However, the movement of your shoulders should not be excessive – movement should only occur around your shoulder.

SHOULDER SHRUG

Dumbbell

Universal

Muscles used: trapezius

Suggested reps: 8-12

Type of movement: single joint

Notes:

- Use an alternating grip or a grip with both palms facing backward when using a barbell or Universal equipment; use a parallel grip with other equipment.
- Keeping your arms and legs straight, pull the resistance up as high as possible trying to touch your shoulders to your ears (as if to say, "I don't know") during the mid-range of each repetition.
- Lower the weight back to the starting position at the completion of each rep to ensure a proper stretch.

- Don't roll your shoulders as you perform this exercise.
- Avoid throwing the resistance by using your legs or by swinging your upper torso back and forth – movement should only occur around your shoulder.
- You can use wrist straps if you have difficulty maintaining your grip.

UPRIGHT ROW

Barbell

Universal

Muscles used: trapezius, biceps, forearms

Suggested reps: 6-10

Type of movement: multiple joint

Notes:

- Your hands should be spaced about eight to ten inches apart.
- Raise the resistance up until your hands are almost shoulder level during the mid-range of each repetition. Your elbows should be slightly higher than your hands in this position.
- Lower the resistance back to the starting position (arms fully extended) at the end of each rep to provide a proper stretch.

- It is biomechanically advantageous to keep the bar as close to your body as possible when performing this movement.
- Avoid throwing the resistance by using your legs or by swinging your upper torso back and forth – movement should only occur around your shoulder and elbow.
- You can use wrist straps if you have difficulty maintaining your grip.
- Upright rows may be inadvisable if you have shoulder impingement.

BICEP CURL

Dumbbell

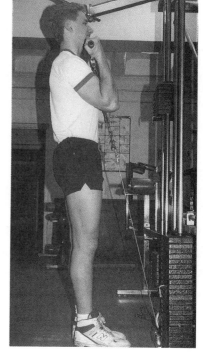

Universal

Muscles used: biceps, forearms

Suggested reps: 6-10

Type of movement: single joint

Notes:

- Your hands should be spaced about shoulder width apart with your palms up.
- Pull the bar (or handles) below your chin during the mid-range of every repetition.
- Lower the resistance back to the starting position (arms fully extended) at the completion of each rep to provide a proper stretch.

- Avoid using your legs and upper torso to throw the weight – movement should only occur around your elbows.
- This movement may be done unilaterally if you have an elbow injury, a gross strength imbalance or desire a training variation.

TRICEP EXTENSION

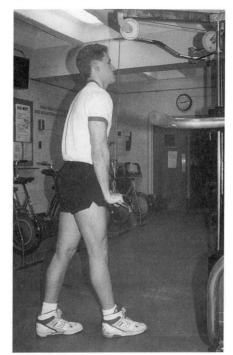

Manual Resistance   **Universal**

Muscles used: triceps

Suggested reps: 6-10

Type of movement: single joint

Notes:

- This exercise can be performed laying supine, sitting upright or standing upright.
- Your hands should be spaced about 4 to 6 inches apart.
- Push the bar, handles or movement arm by extending your arms during the midrange of each repetition. Keep your upper arms perpendicular to the floor throughout the exercise – movement should only occur around your elbow.

- Lower the resistance to the starting position (arms bent) at the end of each rep to ensure a proper stretch.
- This movement may be done unilaterally if you have an elbow injury, a gross strength imbalance or desire a training variation.

WRIST FLEXION

Nautilus

Universal

Dumbbell

Muscles used: wrist flexors

Suggested reps: 8-12

Type of movement: single joint

Notes:

- Your hands should be spaced about 4 to 6 inches apart (palms up) with your thumbs underneath the bar alongside your fingers. Your forearms can be positioned directly over your upper legs or flat on the bench (between your legs). Your forearms should be roughly parallel to the floor. Lean forward slightly so that the angle between your upper and lower arms is 90 degrees or less. Your wrists should be over your kneecaps (or over the edge of the bench if you've placed your forearms there).
- Pull the bar up as high as possible during the mid-range of each repetition by bending your wrists.

- Lower the resistance back to the starting position at the end of each rep to ensure a proper stretch.
- Avoid using your legs and upper torso to throw the weight – movement should only occur around your wrists.
- This movement may be done unilaterally if you have a wrist injury, a gross strength imbalance or desire a training variation.

WRIST EXTENSION

Dumbbell

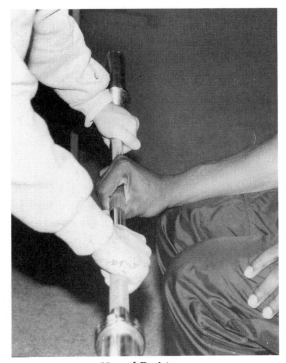

Manual Resistance

Muscles used: wrist extensors

Suggested reps: 8-12

Type of movement: single joint

Notes:

- Grasp the dumbbell, bar or handle with a palms down grip. Your forearm can be positioned directly over your upper leg or flat on the bench (between your legs). Your forearm should be roughly parallel to the floor. Lean forward slightly so that the angle between your upper and lower arm is 90 degrees or less. Your wrist should be over your kneecap (or over the edge of the bench if you've placed your forearm there).
- Pull the weight up as high as possible during the mid-range of each repetition by bending your wrist.

- Lower the resistance back to the starting position at the end of each rep to provide a proper stretch.
- Avoid using your legs and upper torso to throw the weight – movement should only occur around your wrist.
- This exercise is more comfortable when it performed unilaterally.

SIT-UP

Nautilus

Universal

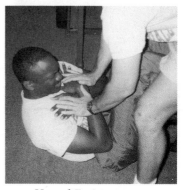

Manual Resistance

Muscles used: rectus abdominis

Suggested reps: 8-12

Type of movement: single joint

Notes:

- If you're doing this exercise using manual resistance, lie flat on the floor and place the backs of your legs on a bench or a stool; if you're doing this exercise on a Universal station, lie down on a sit-up board and place your feet underneath the roller pads. In either case, the angle between your upper and lower legs should be about 90 degrees. Fold your arms across your chest and lift your head off the board (or floor). If you're using a Nautilus machine, sit down and place your upper torso against the back pad. Place your feet underneath the roller pads and grasp the handles.

- Pull your torso forward until it is almost to your upper legs in the mid-range position of each repetition.
- Lower yourself (or the weight) back to the starting position at the end of each rep to provide a proper stretch.
- Avoid throwing your arms or snapping your head forward as you do this movement.
- Your knees should always be bent when performing this movement to reduce the stress on your lower back.
- Sit-ups may be inadvisable if you have low back pain.

SIDE BEND

Dumbbell

Universal

Muscles used: obliques

Suggested reps: 8-12

Type of movement: single joint

Notes:

- Hold the weight (or handle) near one side of your body and spread your feet about shoulder width apart. Stand upright and place your free hand against the side of your head.
- Without moving your hips, pull your upper torso laterally (opposite the resistance) in the mid-range of every repetition.

- Lower the weight back to the starting position at the completion of every rep to obtain a proper stretch.
- Avoid bending forward at the waist as you do this movement.
- Side bends may be unadvisable if you have low back pain.

KNEE-UP

Univeral

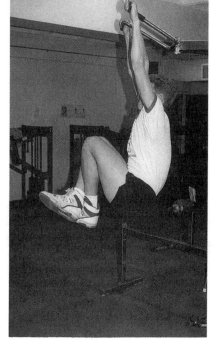

Universal

Muscles used: rectus abdominis (lower), iliopsoas

Suggested reps: 8-12

Type of movement: single joint

Notes:

- Hold onto the bars or handle(s) and cross your ankles.
- Bring your knees as close to your chest as possible in the mid-range of each repetition. Your knees should bend as they are being raised. If you are doing this movement on a sit-up board, your knees should remain bent throughout the entire range of motion.
- Lower your legs back to the starting position at the end of each rep to obtain a proper stretch.
- Avoid throwing your legs up by swinging your hips back and forth.

- If you are unable to do 8 reps in strict form when hanging from a chin bar or dip handles, you should do this movement on the sit-up board. As your strength improves, you can increase the angle of the board thereby making the exercise more difficult. Once the greatest height is no longer a challenge, you can progress to knee-ups from a hanging position.
- Once you can perform 12 reps in strict form from a hanging position, you can increase the workload on your muscles by performing the exercise slower or by having your partner apply resistance to your upper legs.

BACK EXTENSION

Nautilus

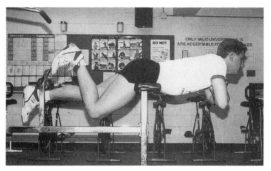

Universal

Muscles used: erector spinae (low back)

Suggested reps: 8-12

Type of movement: single joint

Notes:

- If you're doing this exercise on a Nautilus machine, position yourself so that your legs are underneath the front roller pads and your upper back is against the rear roller pad. Interlock your fingers and place your palms against your mid-section; if you're doing this exercise on a Universal station, position your pelvis on top of the rectangular hip pad. Place your left foot underneath the roller pad and your right foot on top of the foot pedal. Allow your upper torso to hang straight down over the edge of the hip pad and fold your arms across your chest.

- Extend your upper torso backward during the mid-range of each repetition. On the Universal station, don't raise your torso above a point that is parallel to the floor.

- Lower the weight (or yourself) back to the starting position at the end of each rep to provide a proper stretch.

- Avoid throwing your upper torso or snapping your head backward as you do this movement.

- Back extensions may be unadvisable if you have low back pain.

4 SPECIAL CONSIDERATIONS FOR YOUR PROGRAM DESIGN

Your strength program should be geared to your likes and dislikes in terms of exercise selection and equipment preference. This chapter will show you how to structure and fine-tune your own personalized program using the ten strength training principles detailed in Chapter 2 in conjunction with the exercises described in Chapter 3.

PROGRAM OUTLINE

Remember, you should perform one movement for your hips, hamstrings, quadriceps, calves/dorsi flexors, biceps, triceps, forearms, abdominals and lower back. Because your shoulder joint allows freedom of movement in a variety of directions, 2 exercises should be selected for your chest, back (your "lats") and shoulders. Therefore, a program for basketball consists of about 15 exercises during each strength workout.

Occasionally, you may wish to perform an additional movement to emphasize a particular bodypart. That's okay, as long as your strength gains continue. If your strength begins to level off in an exercise, it's probably due to a catabolic effect from performing too many exercises. In addition, too much emphasis on one bodypart may eventually produce abnormal development or create a muscle imbalance which can predispose you to an injury. For example, too many chest exercises may lead to a round-shouldered appearance; too much work on your quadriceps may make you susceptible to a hamstring pull.

Antagonists

How do you know if you're doing too much work for one bodypart and not enough for another? Your muscles are arranged on your body in opposing positions, such as flexors-extensors, abductors-adductors and so on. As an example, your biceps flex (or bend) your arm at the elbow and your triceps extend (or straighten) your arm at the elbow. When one muscle acts in opposition to another, it is referred to as an antagonist. In addition to your biceps-triceps pairing, other antagonistic partnerships include your hip abductors-hip adductors, hamstrings-quadriceps, calves-dorsi flexors, chest-back, anterior deltoid-posterior deltoid, forearm flexors-forearm extensors and abdominals-lower back. In short, your program should not emphasize certain muscle groups without also addressing their antagonistic counterparts in some fashion.

59

Types of Movements

Essentially, there are two types of exercise movements: primary and compound. A primary movement (also known as a simple or single joint movement) involves a range of motion around only one joint. The advantage of a primary movement is that it usually provides muscle isolation. A good example is a pullover in which your upper arm rotates around your shoulder joint thereby isolating your upper back muscles.

A secondary movement (also known as a compound or multiple joint movement) involves ranges of motion around more than one joint. For instance, during a lat pulldown, there is rotation around both your shoulder and your elbow joints – your upper back pulls your upper arm backward around your shoulder joint and your bicep bends your arm at the elbow joint. There's even some work being done at your wrist joint by your forearm flexors to maintain your grip on the bar. Compound exercises are advantageous because you can work relatively large amounts of muscle mass in one movement.

Whenever you do two exercises for a particular bodypart (i.e. your chest, back and shoulders), one of your selections should be a multiple joint movement and the other should be a single joint movement. Why one of each?

Compound movements have a distinct disadvantage because they generally have a "weak link." When a person fatigues in a multiple joint exercise it's because the resistance was filtered through a smaller, weaker muscle which exhausts well before the larger and stronger muscle has received a sufficient workload. In an exercise like the aforementioned lat pulldown, your biceps are the smaller muscle and, therefore, will fatigue long before your upper back. Your grip strength may even be the first to go! So, your biceps and forearms get a pretty good workout but your lats – which you are really trying to exercise – get very little workload. Therefore, if you were to select two multiple joint movements for any major muscle, your smaller muscle structures would get absolutely blasted.

On the one hand, a primary movement is superior to a compound movement because it allows you to isolate a large muscle without being limited by the strength of a small muscle. On the other hand, a compound movement is superior to a primary movement because it exercises a larger amount of muscle mass. As you can see, both primary and compound movements have advantages and disadvantages. This does not mean that it would be totally wrong to do two multiple joint movements for the same bodypart. However, your routine will be more efficient and productive if a single joint movement is selected to offset the limitations of a multiple joint movement.

Composite List of Exercise Selections

BODYPART	SELECTIONS	EXERCISE	REPS	EQUIPMENT	PG
Hips	1	Deadlift	10-15	BDT	26
		Leg Press	10-15	NPU	27
		Hip Abduction	8-12	MNU	28
		Hip Adduction	8-12	MNU	29
Upper Leg	2	Leg Curl	8-12	MNPU	30
		Leg Extension	8-12	MNPU	31
Lower Leg	1	Calf Raise	8-12	DNPU	32
		Dorsi Flexion	8-12	MP	33
Chest	2	Bench Press	6-10	BDMNPU	34
		Incline Press	6-10	BDNPU	35
		Decline Press	6-10	BDNPU	36
		Bent Arm Fly	6-10	DMNP	37
		Dip	6-10	GNPU	38
Back	2	Lat Pulldown	6-10	MNPU	39
		Seated Row	6-10	MNPU	40
		Bent Over Row	6-10	DM	41
		Pullover	6-10	DNP	42
		Chin	6-10	GNU	43
Shoulders	2	Shoulder Press	6-10	BDMNPU	44
		Lateral Raise	6-10	DMNPU	45
		Front Raise	6-10	DMU	46
		Bent Over Raise	6-10	DMPU	47
		Shoulder Shrug	8-12	BDNPTU	48
		Upright Row	6-10	BDMPU	49
Arms	2	Bicep Curl	6-10	BDMNU	50
		Tricep Extension	6-10	BDMNU	51
Forearms	1	Wrist Flexion	8-12	BDMNU	52
		Wrist Extensions	8-12	DMU	53
		Situp	8-12	MNU	54
Abdominals	1	Side Bend	8-12	DNU	55
		Knee-up	8-12	U	56
Lower Back	1	Back Extension	8-12	NU	57

EQUIPMENT CODES:

B = Barbell
D = Dumbbell
G = Gravitron
M = Manual Resistance

N = Nautilus
P = Plate-loading
T = Trap Bar
U = Universal

Sequence

Remember to exercise your muscles from largest to smallest: hips, legs (hamstrings, quadriceps and calves or dorsi flexors), upper torso (chest, back and shoulders), arms (biceps, triceps and forearms), abdominals and lower back.

It is especially important not to exercise your arms before exercising your upper torso or your legs before exercising your hips. It was noted earlier that multiple joint movements require the use of smaller, weaker muscles to assist in the exercise. (As a rule of thumb, your arms are the weak link when performing compound movements for your upper body and your legs are the weak link when performing compound movements for your hips.) So, if you fatigue your smaller muscles first, you'll weaken an already weak link, thereby limiting the workload placed on your larger, more powerful muscles and restrict the potential for their development. Therefore, avoid training your smaller muscles before your larger muscles.

Exercise Options

To assist you in designing routines, a composite list of the exercises detailed in Chapter 3 appears on the previous page. Naturally, your options may differ based upon your available equipment. It would be next to impossible to list exercises for every manufacturer's equipment. However, many companies market products that are quite similar to Nautilus, Universal and plate-loading equipment in terms of design and function; barbells and dumbbells are fairly standard and are usually available at most high schools, universities and fitness centers. Finally, manual resistance exercises are always an option, provided that you have a partner.

Based on the information contained in this and the 2 previous chapters, 2 sample workouts have been constructed and follow. As you can see, a strength training routine can take almost an infinite number of forms. The only limits are your available equipment and your imagination.

Two Sample Routines

SAMPLE ROUTINE #1	SAMPLE ROUTINE #2
Leg Press (N)	Deadlift (T)
Leg Curl (P)	Leg Curl (N)
Leg Extension (M)	Leg Extension (U)
Calf Raise (U)	Dorsi Flexion (P)
Bench Press (D)	Bent Arm Fly (M)
Bent Arm Fly (N)	Incline Press (B)
Lat Pulldown (U)	Pullover (P)
Pullover (N)	Seated Row (N)
Shoulder Press (B)	Lateral Raise (D)
Lateral Raise (M)	Upright Row (B)
Bicep Curl (D)	Bicep Curl (M)
Tricep Extension (U)	Tricep Extension (N)
Wrist Flexion (U)	Wrist Extension (D)
Knee-up (U)	Sit-up (M)
Back Extension (N)	Back Extension (U)

EQUIPMENT CODES:

B = Barbell   **N** = Nautilus

D = Dumbbell   **P** = Plate-loading

G = Gravitron   **T** = Trap Bar

M = Manual Resistance   **U** = Universal

REHABILITATIVE STRENGTH TRAINING

As much as you prepare for the rigors of basketball, injuries sustained during practices and competition are still an unforeseen and inevitable occurrence. You may also have various "noncontact" injuries such as tendinitis, bursitis, general soreness or other nagging afflictions. Once you are injured, the injured area should be treated by qualified sportsmedicine personnel (i.e. athletic trainers, physical therapists, etc.). However, it's very important to continue some type of strength training whenever possible – even in the event of an injury. This will prevent a significant loss in muscular size and strength. Recall that a muscle begins to lose size and strength if it is not exercised within 48-96 hours of its previous workout. Moreover, the rate of strength loss is most rapid during the first few weeks.

There are several different options and adjustments that you can use in order to continue strength training an injured area or bodypart in a safe, prudent and pain-free manner. It should be noted that these methods are intended for those injuries that aren't viewed as being very serious or extremely painful. As such, make sure that you receive approval from a certified sportsmedical authority before initiating any rehabilitative strength training.

It's very important to continue some type of strength training – even in the event of an injury.

1. Lighten the resistance.

If you want to continue training an injured bodypart, your first step is to reduce the amount of weight being used. Let's suppose that your patellar tendon hurts when you do leg extensions with your normal training weight. Reducing the amount of weight will produce less stress on your tendon and perhaps allow you to perform the exercise in a pain-free manner. The amount that the weight is reduced will depend upon the extent and the nature of your injury.

2. Reduce the speed of movement.

If pain-free exercise is still not possible even after reducing the amount of weight, your next move would be to slow down the speed of movement. This may involve raising the weight in about 4 to 8 seconds instead of the traditional 1 to 2 seconds. Reducing the speed of movement will decrease the amount of stress placed on a given joint. Slowing down the speed of movement will also necessitate using a reduced amount of weight thereby lowering the stress even further.

3. Change the exercise angle.

If pain persists during certain exercises involving an injured bodypart, you can try to change the angle at which you perform the movement. This option can be used with many exercises for your upper body – especially those that involve your shoulder joint. Let's say that you have slight shoulder pain when doing a supine bench press. In some cases, if the angle of the bench is changed to either an incline or a decline there will be less stress on the shoulder joint. Likewise, some people experience pain when performing a shoulder press with the bar positioned behind the head. The pain is usually alleviated when performing a shoulder press with the bar in front of the head.

Another exercise which may exacerbate shoulder pain is a behind-the-neck lat pulldown with an overhand grip. Often, the pain is characterized as a tightness or a pinching in the shoulder joint. Generally, the discomfort can be lessened by changing the angle of the pull. This is accomplished by grasping the bar with your palms facing your torso and pulling the bar to your upper chest instead of behind your neck.

4. Use a different grip.

In the case of the shoulder joint, many times there is less stress if a different grip is used. Again, let's say that you have slight pain when doing an exercise such as a bench press. It is quite possible that there will be a significant reduction in pain by simply changing the grip from that used with a barbell to a parallel grip using dumbbells. It should be noted that any exercise that can be performed with a barbell can also be performed with dumbbells. As such, you have an option for varying your grip used in movements for every major muscle group in your upper torso.

5. Perform different exercises.

Yet another option is to perform different exercises that us the same muscle groups. For instance, if you simply cannot perform a lat pulldown without experiencing pain or discomfort then perhaps a different exercise can be used that works the same muscles in a pain-free manner. In this case, you can substitute a seated row or a bent over row to involve the same muscles as a lat pulldown, namely the upper back, biceps and forearms.

6. Limit the range of motion.

There's a possibility that pain occurs only at certain points in the range of motion such as the starting or the mid-range position of the movement. In either case, you can restrict that exercise's range of movement. For example, if pain occurs at the starting position of a movement, then you should stop short of a full stretch; similarly, if pain occurs at the mid-range position of an exercise, then you should stop short of full muscular contraction. As your injured area heals over a period of time, you can gradually increase your range of motion until you obtain a full, pain-free range of motion.

7. Exercise the good limb.

If all else fails, you can still exercise your unaffected limb. For example, suppose you had knee surgery and, as a result, your left leg was placed in a cast from your mid-thigh to your ankle. Obviously, you would not be able to perform any exercises below your left hip joint. However, you can still strength train the muscles on the right side of your lower body. As a matter of fact, some research has shown that training one side of your body will actually effect the muscles on the other side of your body! Researchers aren't exactly sure why this occurs, but the fact of the matter is that it does occur. This phenomenon has been dubbed as "indirect transfer" or "cross transfer."

8. Exercise unaffected bodyparts.

Even though you may not be able to exercise an injured area due to an unreasonable amount of pain or discomfort, you can still perform movements for your uninjured bodyparts. So, if you have a knee injury you can still perform exercises for your entire upper torso – assuming, of course, that the exercises are done sitting or lying and not standing! Likewise, if you have a shoulder injury, you can still train the muscles of your lower body.

OVERCOMING THE STRENGTH "PLATEAU"

Periodically, you'll reach a point in your training when your strength gains have leveled off or "plateaued." Quite often, this is a result of overtraining – you are performing entirely too much work, which causes your muscular system to be overstressed. In effect, the demands have exceeded your recovery ability. In this case, you simply need to reduce the volume of work you are doing in the weight room.

Sometimes, however, your strength will plateau as a result of performing the same routines over and over again each session for long periods of time. In these instances, the workout has become a form of unproductive manual labor that is monotonous, dull and unchallenging.

This can be prevented by varying or changing your workouts. You can do an entirely different workout during each of your 3 weekly sessions, such as Workout "A" on Mondays, Workout "B" on Wednesdays and Workout "C" on Fridays. Workouts can be changed on a week-to-week basis. Or, you can simply change 1 or 2 aspects of your workout as needed in order to inject a little pizazz back into your strength program.

You'll know if you have begun to level off simply by checking your workout card. But review your card carefully. If you appear to have plateaued in a certain movement, you must consider your performance in earlier exercises of that workout. For example, suppose you did 10 reps with 120 pounds on leg extensions for 5 consecutive workouts. At first glance, it doesn't seem as if your quadriceps have gotten stronger, but what if your leg press increased from 250 pounds to 275 pounds during those same 5 workouts? That means the load on your hips, hamstrings and quadriceps increased by ten percent, or an average of 2 percent per workout. Therefore, your quads were increasingly more pre-fatigued each time prior to performing your leg extensions. In this case, there's little doubt that your quads did get stronger. In fact, simply being able to duplicate your past performances on the leg extensions would actually be quite a feat, although that would not be readily apparent. Similarly, if your weight on the bicep curl levels off, it's possible that you're using increasingly heavier weights with your biceps somewhere in your workout – perhaps during lat pulldowns, seated rows or upright rows. So, you must take this into consideration when determining whether you have indeed reached a plateau.

You won't be able to improve your performance in every exercise from one workout to the next. However, you should notice gradual strength gains in all your exercises over the course of about 4 or 5 workouts. Failure to make a progression in an exercise (in resistance or repetitions) by this time is your signal to change some aspect of your routine. There are several ways that this may be accomplished.

1. Rearrange the order.

One of the easiest ways to modify your workout is to rearrange the order in which you perform exercises for a particular bodypart. Suppose, for example, your shoulder strength seems to have reached a plateau. If you've been doing an upright row followed by a shoulder press, you can switch these 2 movements, performing the shoulder press first and the upright row next.

Remember, you must adjust your weights whenever you vary the order of exercises. Using the previous example, let's say you normally use 90 pounds in the upright row followed quickly by a shoulder press with 100 pounds. If the order of exercises is changed (i.e. the shoulder press is done first), your shoulder musculature will be relatively fresh for the shoulder press and, therefore, you would now be able to handle more resistance. However, you must reduce your usual weight in the upright row, since your deltoids will be more fatigued than usual from performing the shoulder press beforehand.

As a variation, many exercises may be done unilaterally, or with one limb at a time.

An additional possibility is to exercise your muscle groups in a different sequence. Instead of going from chest to back to shoulders, you might start with your back exercises, then proceed to your shoulder movements and finish off with your chest area. So, an upper torso routine of bench press, bent arm fly, lat pulldown, pullover, shoulder press and lateral raise could be changed to pullover, lat pulldown, lateral raise, shoulder press, bent arm fly and bench press. In fact, these six exercises alone could be rearranged for 720 different routines! Once again, any time you rearrange your sequence of exercises, you'll need to adjust the levels of resistance.

2. Change the modality.

Another way to vary your training is to change the modality or equipment used. For instance, if you plateau on the bench press, you can perform a similar movement using different equipment. The previous chapter specified six distinct bench press modalities using a barbell, dumbbells, manual resistance, Nautilus, plate-loading and Universal Gym equipment. Obviously, the extent to which you can change the modality depends on the equipment that is available.

3. Alternate the exercises.

A third means of varying your workout is to alternate the exercises that involve the same muscle group(s). For example, the bench press, incline press, decline press and dip are all multiple joint chest movements that also exercise your shoulders and triceps. If you peak in one of these exercises, you can simply substitute another movement which employs the same musculature. Once again, the availability of equipment will determine how much the exercises may be alternated.

4. Vary the repetition.

A final option is to vary the manner in which you perform your repetitions. Repetitions can be done at least 5 different ways: bilaterally, unilaterally, negative only, negative accentuated and modified cadence. The traditional way is to do a movement bilaterally, or with both limbs at the same time. However, as a variation, many exercises may also be done unilaterally, or with one limb at a time. An entire set of repetitions may be performed in a negative only manner by having your training partner raise the weight for you while you lower the weight under control in about 6 to 8 seconds per rep. Many machines permit you to do your reps in a negative accentuated fashion in which you raise the weight with both limbs, lower the weight with one limb, raise the weight with both limbs and lower the weight with the other limb. Finally, you can modify the cadence or the speed of movement of your repetitions. For example, instead of performing 12 reps at 6 seconds per rep you could do 7 reps at 10 seconds per rep. Note that in both instances your muscle is under tension for approximately 70 seconds.

IN-SEASON STRENGTH TRAINING

Your strength gains will be minimal during the season, especially as practices become more intense. Although this isn't necessarily cause for alarm, you may have to reduce your workout frequency and the total number of exercises that you perform in the weight room to allow for adequate recovery. In any event, you should understand that the added activity of practices, games and sometimes even traveling will make strength gains difficult to accomplish during the season.

THE SECOND HALF:

CONDITIONING FOR A PURPOSE

In order to compete at your full potential as a basketball player, it's important for you to be as highly conditioned as possible.

5 PHYSIOLOGICAL FUNDAMENTALS OF CONDITIONING

The human body is one of the most remarkable machines on the planet. It's various biological systems (e.g. skeletal, respiratory, circulatory) function separately yet collectively. The depth and scope of this feature is truly amazing and intimidating – just check out the medical section of any library!

In order to compete at your full potential as a basketball player, it's important for you to be as highly conditioned as possible. Because of this, the intent of this chapter is to give you a detailed – yet practical – working knowledge of the different energy systems within your body that are responsible for the conditioning process. Each of your "metabolic pathways" has a main power plant and operates independently. However, they wouldn't be able to function without assistance from each other.

ADENOSINE TRIPHOSPHATE

The energy liberated during the breakdown of food is used to make a chemical compound called adenosine triphosphate, or more simply, ATP. This compound is stored in most living cells – particularly muscle cells – and has an extremely high energy yield. The structure of ATP consists of an adenosine component that is bonded to three chemically-important phosphate groups. The energy from ATP is not necessarily in its make-up, but in the so-called high energy phosphate bonds which hold the compound together. When one of the phosphate bonds is broken – or removed from the rest of the molecule – energy is released. The energy liberated during the breakdown of ATP is your primary – and immediate – source of energy to perform muscular work.

YOUR ENERGY SYSTEMS

Energy is also required to resynthesize (or rebuild) ATP. The energy systems of your body all revolve around one primary function: to reconstruct ATP in order to supply energy so that your muscles can perform physical work. The process by which ATP is put back together involves three different series of chemical reactions. Two of these do not require the presence of oxygen and are termed anaerobic; the other series of reactions can only operate in the existence of oxygen and is labeled aerobic. Your two anaerobic energy systems are the ATP-PC System and Anaerobic Glycolysis; your aerobic source is known as the

Aerobic System. These systems always work together but differ on input, based upon your level of intensity and the duration of your activity.

The ATP-PC System

Your ATP-PC (or Phosphagen) System is a great example of the ability of your systems to furnish energy. In this system, the energy used to rebuild ATP comes from the breakdown of one molecule – phosphocreatine, or PC. PC – like ATP – is basically a chemical substance that is stored in your muscle cells and has a rather high energy yield. Since ATP and PC both contain phosphate groups, they are collectively referred to as "phosphagens." Similar to ATP, PC releases a large amount of energy when its phosphate group is removed. This energy is immediately available and is used to remake ATP. In fact, as quickly as ATP is broken down during muscular efforts, it is continuously remanufactured by the energy released from the breakdown of PC. How much ATP is available from this system? Well, the phosphagen stores in the working muscles would probably be spent after about 10 seconds of all-out exercise, such as sprinting 100 yards. So, the total amount of ATP energy available from the phosphagen system is very limited. However, fast, powerful movements – like dunking the ball and racing down the court – could not be performed without this metabolic system. It's no surprise then that this system provides energy for exercise of very high intensity and brief duration – less than about 30 seconds.

The ability of your ATP-PC System to provide energy – essentially rebuilt ATP – is directly related to the kind of activity or movement that is stressing the system. The time that it takes to replenish ATP is also directly related to the recovery interval between bouts of exercise. This is important to consider when designing a conditioning program, because your workout intensity will be higher if you know your time limits on recovery intervals. Most sports have built-in recovery intervals, whether they are from time-outs or simply because of the intermittent nature of the game. This allows for some replenishment of your all-important ATP stores.

Anaerobic Glycolysis

In your body, carbohydrates are converted to glucose – a simple sugar – which can either be instantly utilized in that form or stored as glycogen in your liver and muscles for later use. The term "glycolysis" means to break down glycogen and, as stated earlier, "anaerobic" basically means without oxygen. Therefore, Anaerobic Glycolysis refers to the breakdown of glycogen in the absence of oxygen. When glycogen is broken down, energy is released and is used to reconstruct ATP. However, since oxygen isn't required, the breakdown of glycogen is only partial. This incomplete breakdown of glycogen leaves an end product called lactic acid – which is why Anaerobic Glycolysis is often referred to as the Lactic Acid System. When you burn a log you are always left with ash as a waste product. Similarly, lactic acid is the glycolytic ash of the body's anaerobic pathway. Lactic acid is truly an inhibitor for Anaerobic Glycolysis. In fact, your muscles and blood can only tolerate about 2 to 2½ ounces of lactic acid before fatigue sets in!

Anaerobic Glycolysis – with a helping hand from your ATP-PC System – is responsible for supplying ATP for all maximal efforts that last between approximately 1 to 1 ½ minutes, such as sprinting between about 440 and 880 yards. In other words, the first few minutes of exercise depend upon the body's ability to replenish ATP without the use of oxygen. The resynthesis of ATP is quite rapid but, without the presence of oxygen, is somewhat limited.

The Aerobic System

The Aerobic System is the last one in the chemical chain of command for energy production. In the Aerobic System, glycogen is once again broken down to release energy used to rebuild ATP. Because oxygen is used in this process, the breakdown of glycogen is complete. Your Aerobic System is one that can be continuous because no fatiguing by-products – like lactic acid – are formed in the presence of oxygen. This particular system does produce two products: carbon dioxide and water. However, carbon dioxide is continually removed by the blood and carried to the lungs where it is exhaled; water is actually useful in the cell itself. So, glycolytic reactions occur both in the aerobic and anaerobic systems – the difference is that lactic acid isn't formed when sufficient oxygen is available. Another feature of your Aerobic System is that it can also break down both proteins and fats to free energy to remake ATP, while anaerobically only carbohydrates can be used.

This process of rebuilding ATP aerobically occurs in specialized areas of the muscle cell called the mitochondria. This area has been referred to as the "powerhouse" of the cell because of the amount of the energy that can be produced there. Muscle cells are usually very rich with mitochondria.

The actual time that aerobic glycolysis begins differs among many individuals. Some believe aerobic metabolism occurs in as little as three minutes; others feel that a minimum of twelve minutes is needed in order to activate this system. However, a minimum of twelve minutes is needed for training benefits to occur. For actual aerobic glycolysis to begin, it would have to start after the anaerobic system has been exhausted and lactic acid begins to accumulate. The minimum running distance would be at least a half mile run. Remember, continual activity is the key to aerobic training.

Basketball has an aerobic component since anaerobic movements are performed over a fairly long period of time.

THE ENERGY CONTINUUM

So far, we have seen how the body's aerobic and anaerobic processes produce energy for muscular work. The body's ability to provide ATP is directly related to the intensity and the duration of the activity that is to be performed. On the one end of the continuum, is your anaerobic ATP-PC System which produces energy for short-term, high-intensity efforts and, on the other end is your Aerobic System which supplies ATP for long-term, low-intensity work. In between these two extremes are gray zones in which the anaerobic and aerobic systems are blended together. There are many sports and activities which require a mixture of both systems, such as running ½ to 1 mile, rowing 1 to 1 ¼ miles, swimming 220 to 440 yards, wrestling 2 minute periods and boxing 3 minute rounds. The need for a particular energy system fluctuates as the time and intensity requirements change for a specific activity. Both aerobic and anaerobic systems contribute some ATP during physical performance, with one system always contributing more. The game of basketball – like most team sports – is primarily anaerobic because it consists of a series of short, explosive movements. However, basketball also has an aerobic component since the anaerobic movements are required over a fairly long period of time. Therefore, energy is needed from both the anaerobic and aerobic systems. If you can improve these systems through conditioning then you can also improve your performance potential.

THE ENGINE FOR THE SYSTEM

As you can see, the presence of oxygen and its ability to be delivered directly effects the energy systems of your body. Through the energy continuum, your body's energy systems work in phases on a progressive scale. When that scale changes, your body must modify the way it generates energy. As the time of an activity increases, the continuum shifts away from anaerobic work toward aerobic work. This metabolic shift requires your heart to increase its blood flow. With an increased blood flow comes oxygen-rich blood which, in turn, feeds your aerobic system.

Your "Muscular Pump"

Your heart is the main muscle in your body and is the primary driving force behind your three energy systems. This "muscular pump" can be broken down into left and right halves. Each half of your heart consists of two chambers – an atrium and a ventricle. The left half of your heart pumps blood to your body tissues, such as your skeletal muscles; the right half of your heart sends blood to your lungs.

Like all muscle tissue, your heart will hypertrophy with training. Specifically, its ventricular cavity becomes larger and its ventricular wall becomes thicker. This permits your heart to accept more blood and expel it more powerfully.

Indeed, as your heart becomes a better conditioned muscle, its ability to circulate blood also improves. In particular, two aspects are enhanced: stroke volume and heart rate. Stroke volume is the amount of blood pumped by the heart per beat and is usually measured in milliliters; heart rate is simply the number of times your heart beats in one minute. Stroke volume can only reach a certain point before it levels off. As your level of conditioning improves, the point at which stroke volume reaches a steady-state value becomes higher. Your resting heart rate will also be lowered as a direct result of training. A slower heart rate coupled with a larger stroke volume indicates an efficient circulatory system. This is true because your heart won't beat as often for a given cardiac output. Knowing that the heart can pump more blood per beat and needs less beats to function, you can see that proper conditioning will greatly increase the efficiency of the pump that drives your system.

Your "Respiratory Pump"

Along with generating blood flow throughout your body, your heart also plays an important part in everyday respiration. Respiration is both interior and exterior. Interior respiration is the exchange of gases – namely oxygen and carbon dioxide – with the blood and tissues of your body. The intercostal muscles of your rib cage and your diaphragm muscle in conjunction with the natural changes of pressures within your body, allows an open trade of these two gases. As venous blood passes through your lungs, it loads oxygen and unloads carbon dioxide (which is disposed of externally). Oxygen and carbon dioxide are also exchanged between your arterial blood and your body tissues. In this case, oxygen is delivered to your tissues and carbon dioxide is picked up by your blood.

The importance of respiration cannot be overemphasized. Along with respiratory balance, this system also regulates the acid-base system of your body. The acid-base system is basically your body's alarm system that signals to you when you can't go any further. As you become more highly conditioned, the levels at which you can eliminate wastes, exchange gases and cushion the metabolically-produced acids becomes greater. Recall that lactic acid is a direct by-product of anaerobic training and is the prime suspect of muscular fatigue. Without the body's ability to provide a system to remove this by-product, your body fluids will become more acidic and disturb the precious acid-base balance. This sends a signal to the brain that no additional work can be done until the situation is corrected. If your body has been adequately trained and conditioned, then the waste products can be removed faster thereby delaying muscular fatigue. If not, your performance must stop until more acceptable levels are reached. Unfortunately, blood lactate will always be created during anaerobic activity. What separates the highly conditioned athletes from the out-of-shape athletes is the degree to which they can tolerate it and how quickly they can remove it

AEROBIC AND ANAEROBIC MAXIMUMS

Your conditioning maximums are effected by a number of different factors. Perhaps the most important determinant here are your genetic limitations. These inherited characteristics include your limb length, muscle insertion points and predominant muscle fiber type. There's an old saying that sprinters are born and not made. That may be true, but there are really no limitations on your own ability to improve against yourself.

Your maximum aerobic capacity would seem to be the total amount of oxygen that you can inhale or exhale per breath. This is called tidal volume and can range anywhere from 0.5 to 3.0 liters of oxygen, depending upon whether you are in a resting or an active state. Of greatest concern is the amount of oxygen that is taken in and then utilized by the active muscles. This amount is known as your Maximum Oxygen Consumption or Maximum Oxygen Uptake (VO_2 max). This has become a standard by which people have measured their body's response to aerobic training and their improvements. Remember, since your body can store only a limited amount of oxygen, it is very critical that its oxygen-supplying system is able to handle great workloads. As your body continues to exercise, it will eventually reach a limit for oxygen delivery. This level is your max VO_2. Your VO_2 is directly affected by body size, age and your current conditioning level. Someone with greater body mass has a greater need for oxygen during aerobic work than someone with less body mass. Also, as you get older, your body composition has a tendency to change – your muscle mass decreases and your body fat increases thereby effecting your oxygen uptake.

With VO_2 maximums, the amount of oxygen used by the system is being measured. This method is effective, but a better way may be to measure the point during training that your blood lactate – the lactic acid which has accumulated in your bloodstream – begins to build up. This measurement is an expression of the intensity of exercise in relation to your physiological limits. With steady-state exercise, your blood lactate begins to rise. When your "anaerobic threshold" has been reached, there is a steep increase in your blood lactate. This threshold can be gauged against a point on your VO_2 max. For example, suppose your blood lactate levels are monitored while you perform a max VO_2 test. At some point during the test, your lactate level will rise sharply. This can be noted by observing the point during the VO_2 test where your level rose – such as an 85 percent level of your Max VO_2. The higher the percentage that you achieve before your lactate rises sharply, the longer you can exercise before metabolic factors limit your performance. Fatigue will eventually set in as more muscle glycogen is utilized and waste products are broken down that cannot be removed at a pace that equals accumulation.

The term "anaerobic maximum" in itself seems puzzling. Unlike aerobic training where the whole intent is long-term but somewhat low in intensity, anaerobic work is very short-term but very high in intensity. It's difficult to devise a valid maximum test which is done over a very short time span. On the other hand, it is critical that some guidelines and yardsticks be established in order to show improvements in anaerobic conditioning. Any work done anaerobically must fall into a time guideline of between one second and three minutes. This leaves some leeway as far as designing an anaerobic test. Some proven tests that fall within these time requirements would be a 10 x 40 yard test (i.e. a series of ten 40 yard sprints) and a 30-second all-out sprint test on a stationary bicycle with descending power levels. For basketball, something more suitable might be a series of "30-second suicide" drills or several "60-second width" sprints. (The specifics of these tests are described in Chapter 8.) Practicality is the key message here. For instance, performing a 10 x 1-second sprint test really doesn't apply to the sport of basketball! When designing a conditioning test, it's necessary to closely correlate the physical ability or capacity being measured by the test you plan to conduct. This can be done more accurately by carefully watching the sport and determining both the distances and the times that are required for various tasks or skills – such as running the length or width of the court. So, any anaerobic test for basketball should consider using times and distances that do not deviate from that fact. As you'll soon see, the most important thing you can do with any conditioning test or drill work will revolve around one word: specificity.

THE HUMAN "MACHINE"

As you've seen, your body is driven by a series of different systems which work collectively as well as separately. An automobile also has different operating systems, such as its air conditioning, transmission, and exhaust systems. All systems have one thing in common: they provide an autonomous service, yet cannot function without each other. Not to compare the human body to a mechanical device, but the similarities are striking. The biggest difference that the human "machine" has over any other machine is its ability to adapt and improve through added stress. We know that with appropriate levels of stress provided through exercise, the systems of the human machine will improve its functional ability and perform more efficiently. This cannot be said for all other machines which usually break down with additional stress. Proper, progressive conditioning will help you become a better athlete by making all of your body's independent systems work better and together as a unit.

6 GENERAL CONDITIONING: AEROBIC

One of the most difficult things a coach or athlete has to do is to interpret what science has said and apply that information in a practical manner to develop a program. Though complicated at times in how it effects the body, aerobic training has some very specific yet simple guidelines which must be followed closely. There are many questions that must be addressed when trying to include aerobic training in your year-round program: Where is aerobic training most helpful? What style of aerobic conditioning is most beneficial for the basketball player? How much of an emphasis should aerobic training receive? The purpose of this chapter is to answer these and other questions.

GENETICS

The biggest factor that impacts upon an athlete's ability to perform well during aerobic training is genetics. The "genetic profile" of an endurance athlete differs greatly from that of a basketball player. A good example of this is to consider an inherited characteristic, such as the predominant muscle fiber type. Although there are at least 17 different subclassifications, muscle fibers can be categorized into two main types: fast twitch (FT) and slow twitch (ST). The fatigue-resistant ST fibers are better suited for prolonged, endurance activities. Compared to ST fibers, FT fibers generate huge amounts of force and, therefore, are responsible for rapid, powerful movements. Athletes that have a high percentage of ST muscle fibers would be successful at activities that require a large amount of endurance such as long distance running; those that have a high percentage of FT muscle fibers would be more competitive at sports that specify quick, explosive actions like those found in basketball. Your actual percentage and distribution pattern of these two fiber types is established during your development soon after birth and remains relatively constant for the rest of your life.

Limb length is another genetic factor which may limit the amount of work that a basketball athlete is able to accomplish aerobically. If you compare two athletes who are 5'8" and 6'8", common sense indicates that there is a 12 inch difference in skeletal height between the two. The odds are that there's also a disparity in limb length. Suppose both of these athletes are measured aerobically while pedaling on a bike for a period of 25 minutes. If they both pedal the same distance, the 6'8" athlete will have done more work because his or her muscles and joints were exercised through greater ranges of movement. As the range of motion increases, the muscles utilize more glycogen which will eventually require more calories to fuel the body. The shorter-limbed individual has inherited a biomechanical leverage advantage and, in theory, can perform the same amount of work in the same amount of time with less effort.

So, leverage-wise and fiber type-wise a longer-limbed person can be at a distinct disadvantage in aerobic activities. This might lead someone to ask, "Why bother to train aerobically?" The answer lies in the system that drives the athlete: The more finely-tuned your aerobic system becomes, the better your anaerobic system will be able to function. Since basketball is highly anaerobic, athletes must have their aerobic system running as efficiently and as effectively as possible to provide physiological support for their anaerobic system.

Besides this very important fact, aerobic training assists the body in several other ways. Aerobic training will help maintain your percentage of body fat at an acceptable level when used in conjunction with proper dieting. Additionally, athletes with a low capacity for endurance succumb to fatigue quicker than athletes with high endurance levels – regardless of what sport they participate in. Indeed, your heart and all its systems function more productively through general aerobic conditioning.

AEROBIC GUIDELINES

By definition, aerobic training is any type of activity that is continuous in nature and takes place for a sustained period of time. As noted in chapter 5, aerobic glycolysis may begin as early as 3 minutes into exercise and last until exhaustion has set in. The general consensus among most fitness professionals is that an exercise must last a minimum of 12 minutes in order for aerobic training benefits to be gained. Some people might recommend that a minimum of 20 minutes is needed, while others might suggest even higher. Twelve minutes is adequate, but the biggest determining factor in the duration of training is your level of intensity. To gain the largest benefits from aerobic conditioning, it's sometimes better to sacrifice your level of intensity for exercise duration. As you approach the 25 to 35 minute mark during your training, more fat is being oxidized and your heart is working harder for a longer amount of time. Attempting to train with too much intensity aerobically may cause you to approach your anaerobic zone. The result is that you might not collect the optimal benefits from aerobic conditioning.

The intensity at which you train aerobically can be quantified by examining your exercise heart rate. Therefore, you can work at certain percentages of your maximum heart rate (max HR) and be quite accurate in measuring intensity. An estimate of your age-predicted max HR can be obtained by simply subtracting your age from 220. For instance, a twenty year old basketball player would have an age-predicted max HR of 200 beats per minute [220 - 20 = 200]. Once you have defined your max HR, you can determine your training heart rate zone rather easily. Maximum aerobic benefits begin to develop by training at a level of at least 75% of your max HR. It goes without saying that you wouldn't be able to train at 100% of your max HR for a substantial amount of time! Science has shown that levels of as much as 80-85% of max HR can be reached and held for significant lengths of time. Based on these percentages (i.e. 75% and 85%), a 20 year old basketball player must train aerobically with a level of intensity that elevates his or her heart rate somewhere between 150 to 170 beats per minute (bpm). [200 bpm × .75 = 150 bpm; 200 bpm × .85 = 170 bpm.] However, sustaining a heart rate of 150 to 170 bpm is a broad range for an athlete to maintain. More specific guidance could be to train at increasing percentages of a max HR for a prescribed period of time, such as 75% of max HR for 5 minutes, 80% for 10 minutes and 85% for 5 minutes. In this manner, an athlete must continually increase either the pace or the resistance on whatever type of aerobic modality being used in order to raise the heart rate to a desirable level of intensity.

Your heart rate can be easily measured at several different sites on your body. There are several heart rate monitors that are available commercially that will give you a reasonably accurate reading of your heart rate. However, the easiest and cheapest way is to measure your own heart rate. This can be done by locating your pulse at either your carotid artery (in your neck) or your radial artery (in your wrist). Once you've begun heavy exercise, your carotid and radial arteries will be easy to find. Simply place the tips of your index and middle fingers over one of these sites. When you locate your heart beat, count your pulse for 10 seconds. Then, multiply that number by 6 and you will have your heart rate for one minute.

As you continue to train, your ability to reach and maintain a higher training heart rate will become easier. As such, it's important to note that aerobic training – like strength training – needs to be progressive for further improvements.

CROSS-TRAINING

An overload must be applied to your aerobic system at each workload or plateaus will occur. When you are dealing with continuous training – which may be monotonous at times – it's easy to level off. For this reason, it's meaningful to keep accurate records of data from your last workout so that you may improve upon it. There are many factors that you can manipulate when trying to prevent your aerobic training from becoming stale, such as the duration of the workout, the frequency of training and your intensity levels. Changing modalities is an excellent way to overcome plateaus in aerobic training. Fortunately, a characteristic of aerobic training is that it allows a large degree of flexibility in terms of exercise selection. Remember, you are looking to train your heart. How you do it is not as critical as your intensity and time of activity. Your heart won't know if you ride a bike one day and climb stairs the next.

The need for using different modalities has led to the evolution of a system of conditioning known as cross-training. This is a style of training that was originally developed for triathletes who found it necessary to work on more than one skill while still exercising the systems of their body. The inherent nature of the triathlon dictates that you must be strong on wheels, in water and on land. Not only do you need proficiency at biking, swimming and running, but you must have the aerobic ability to endure several hours of virtually uninterrupted activity. Recreational athletes have taken this philosophy and restructured their sometimes boring aerobic workouts. For example, instead of taking one 45 minute aerobic dance class, a person might do three different activities in that same time frame, such as rowing, stairclimbing and running on the treadmill for 15 minutes each. This method of conditioning allows for variety, while enabling you to train at a higher level of intensity for three shorter periods of time rather than a lower level of intensity for one lengthy period of time. It also permits you to exercise the same muscle groups in a different manner and to concentrate on your weaker areas. Since most people have some type of aerobic training impairment, cross-training allows you to address a specific weakness. Cross-training also prevents mental burnout because your amount of conditioning time is divided into smaller portions.

MODES OF TRAINING

Any activity that is rhythmic in nature and falls within an appropriate level of intensity and time intervals can be considered aerobic exercise. Variety is what makes aerobic training so unique and different. The ability to train the aerobic system in an orthopaedically-safe manner has increased with the arrival of more advanced exercise equipment. In the past, the only real method of aerobic training was to run long distances outdoors. Aerobic training machines, however, allow athletes to train in an almost non-weight-bearing environment. This is significant if you consider the complexion of basketball. Basketball is a quick, explosive sport where repetitive jumping is required in order to be successful. Combining this with constant sprinting on a playing surface – which at times can be very unforgiving – makes basketball very stressful to the joints and support structures of the body. Indeed, every time you take a step you are distributing a force of at least 1-2 times your bodyweight throughout the joints of your body. When running, the force may rise to 2-4 times your bodyweight. The force rises even more dramatically when jumping. If you separate the injuries that are traumatic in nature (ankle sprains, cuts, muscle tears) from the ones that are nontraumatic (stress fractures, tendinitis, bursitis), you'll note that the nontraumatic injuries are usually caused by overuse. This is important to note because every true basketball player is driven to always work hard at his or her game for lengthy periods of time. A system of conditioning that adds unreasonable and undesirable stress to the joints of an athlete's body will have a detrimental impact on your program. Therein lies the beauty of non-weight-bearing aerobic training: You can still gain aerobic conditioning benefits without exposing your body to excessive pounding. When you are on a 12 month training regimen it's essential to train smartly. Utilizing different aerobic modalities allows you to do just that.

There are pros and cons to various aerobic modalities. As with strength training – where training with machines has certain advantages over free weights and vice versa – each aerobic tool has its strong and weak points. No single system of aerobic training is the best. There are some that should be used only during certain times of the year, while others are very basketball-specific. The following is a breakdown of several aerobic modalities with a candid look at both the pros and cons:

Your heart rate can be measured by locating your pulse at your carotid artery (in your neck).

Pool Work

The advent of the pool as a conditioning modality was established by athletic trainers. It was found that exercising in a pool was the only way to maintain or improve the conditioning levels of some injured athletes. The water acted as a cushion that reduced any severe stress on their bones, joints and connective tissue. The pool has since emerged as a new frontier for conditioning healthy, uninjured athletes, particularly basketball players.

Any type of swimming activity requires a great deal of energy from the body's musculature, making this activity a whole body workout. Running and sprinting can also be done in the pool. In this case, the water provides resistance to the body's moving limbs, thereby placing constant tension on the muscles. Anyone who has tried swimming as a conditioning workout will readily agree that the amount of time spent actually swimming during the first few workouts is usually rather low. This is primarily due to two factors. First of all, swimming places a challenging – yet non-weight-bearing – stress on the body. Secondly, swimming is a highly specialized skill that takes a considerable amount of practice to master. If there are any negatives to swimming, it's that swimming is a skill in which some people have perfected more than others. As such, if pool work is prescribed, a lack of swimming skills can interfere with your potential conditioning benefits. Flotation devices – such as an aqua-vest or a simple kick board – can help overcome any shortcoming of swimming skills. Remember, your aerobic training must be continuous and involve your major muscle groups.

Swimming fits both of these requirements. Your swimming doesn't have to be pretty as long as it's effective!

Stationary Bicycles

The stationary bike has long been a mode of exercise for the average individual. The bike – like pool workouts – was introduced to the conditioning scene by the athletic training community. Biking is another classic example of non-weight-bearing exercise, since no actual ground contact is made. Because of this, conditioning can last for long periods of time in an orthopaedically safe manner. For this reason, an exercise bike is usually included in most rehabilitation programs as one of the key protocols used to "recondition" an athlete and expedite his or her return to competition. Exercise bikes are unique modalities to use because they help condition – or recondition – athletes in several different ways. First of all, there's no skill level required for stationary biking because its rotary motion is the same no matter what type of exercise bike you ride. Stationary bikes also allow you to isolate the larger muscle groups of your lower body – the ones that are used predominantly during the game of basketball. Unlike the pool where the water resists your body's movements, biking lets you add enough resistance so that you can simulate pedaling up an incline of various grades. This means that you can perform more basketball-specific work. Bike sprints help you raise and lower your heart rate at your own discretion – all by increasing or decreasing the resistance. The arrival of the new electronically-braked bikes gives the user even easier control. Some of the recent bike models even provide resistance while peddling in reverse which really emphasizes the leg muscles in a way that is similar to backpedaling on the court.

One of the newer innovations is the so-called "recumbent bike." This particular bike positions the user in a car-like bucket seat. Recumbent bikes enhance comfort dramatically compared to traditional, upright pedaling and also decrease the stress on the lumbar spine.

Rowing Machines

Rowing involves just about all your major muscle groups – the hips, legs, low back and the pulling muscles of the upper torso. Exercising continuously using this large amount of muscle mass creates a sizable expenditure of calories. Many rowing machines present digital feedback including the distance rowed, the pace and the estimated caloric consumption. Unfortunately, few companies manufacture a rower that gives a true simulation or feeling of actually pulling an oar through water. Athletes with low back problems should pursue other conditioning modalities. Boredom may also be a problem.

Stairclimbing Machines

The era of stairclimbing machines began in an 8 x 10 foot booth at a Chicago trade show in 1984. Since the latter part of the 1980s, the popularity of these machines has truly come on strong. Stair climbing machines – like the exercise bike – allow greater isolation of the hips and legs. Recent studies have shown that leg strength measured on a leg press has increased when using a stair climbing machine as the main source of lower body exercise. Stair climbing machines are fairly easy to operate and allow for different modes of training, such as continuous or short sprint. Stair climbing also helps to strengthen the lower back isometrically, since those muscles must contract to stabilize the body during this type of activity. One of the problems that arises with this style of training is exercise form. As an athlete becomes exhausted, there's a tendency to hang onto the machine any way possible. This makes the training inefficient and potentially dangerous. Many of the stairclimbing machines that are on the market are of a poor quality and probably won't hold up very long once your power forward gets through with it. Some machines may also predispose the knee to hyperextension at the bottom portion of the movement. Cost is sometimes a prohibiting factor. Some universities and fitness centers simply can't afford a top-of-the-line stairclimbing machine.

Aerobics

Aerobic dance classes – or simply "aerobics" – have skyrocketed in popularity among the general public. In fact, it's a safe bet that an aerobic dance class could be found somewhere practically 24 hours a day! This is another modality to choose from when constructing your year-round conditioning program for basketball. Aerobics were created as an effective way to manage large numbers of people who are seeking the benefits of aerobic training in a pleasant, music-filled atmosphere. Aerobics combine rhythmic dance movements with calisthenics and exercises that are blended together by the instruction of a class leader. Like the previous modalities, aerobic dance has its good and bad points. This type of training can produce an enormous boost in overall conditioning, along with being a tremendous whole body activity. Since classes change with different instructors and the level of the participants, monotony isn't usually an obstacle. Some problems that have recently arisen from aerobics are overtraining and a general wear-and-tear on the body. Participating in classes of 45 to 60 minutes for extended periods of time tends to place an inordinate amount of stress on the joints of the lower body. The so-called "step aerobics" places even greater demands on the knees, shins, ankles and low back and can quickly lead to a variety of overuse injuries if done in excess. The flooring is a very important factor to consider: the softer and more giving the surface, the safer it is. A poor class leader can also mean a loss of optimal training benefits. In general, aerobics can provide an important function in your training program. However, consid-

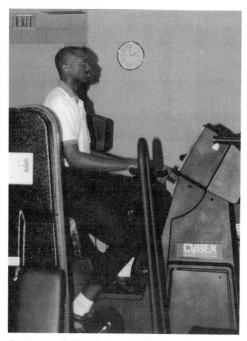

Stationary biking is an excellent non-weight-bearing exercise that can be used for conditioning or rehabilitation.

erations should be given as to how frequently this type of training is used during the year.

Motorized Treadmills

Walking, jogging or running on a motorized treadmill provides exactly the same conditioning benefits as those of its "outdoor" counterparts. The treadmill is also a high calorie user making it an efficient and effective tool for weight management. Treadmills offer fingertip control of the speed and elevation as well as other electronic feedback. Another advantage of a treadmill is that your running can be done in an air conditioned environment that is constant and safe. However, this is probably the most expensive of all aerobic modalities. Many of the other advantages and disadvantages of treadmill running are the same as that of outdoor running.

Distance Running

One of the easiest and least expensive techniques of aerobic training has always been distance running outdoors. Sometimes referred to as "long, slow distance training," this method is perhaps the earliest form of aerobic training. The lack of complications makes distance running so appealing: No special machines, amount of money or other individuals are necessary to gain a productive workout. As long as the time and heart rate (i.e. intensity) qualifications are met, distance running will have a positive influence on your aerobic system. Distance running has its own advantages due to its specific nature. Running to condition yourself is more specific to basketball, since the sport itself involves so much running. Many athletes have even said that the benefits of distance running translate to other types of aerobic training but that the benefits don't really transfer from other aerobic modalities.

Some of the drawbacks with distance running are the same as those of the previous modalities that have already been discussed. For example, an individual who is 6'8" and 240 pounds subjects the body's ligament and tendon support systems to a large amount of stress during long distance running – especially on hard pavement. In fact, a person weighing 240 pounds creates about 480 to

960 pounds of downward force with each footfall – at maybe 1000 footfalls per mile! In addition, anaerobically rich athletes – such as basketball players – aren't particularly known for their distance running!

INTELLIGENT TRAINING

As you can see, there are many methods available for training aerobically. Through careful planning, you can easily avoid overtraining and its accompanying plateaus. Focusing on one area of aerobic training can also lead to overuse injuries. For instance, distance running is an excellent conditioning tool, but seven days of it per week is probably too stressful to the body. On the other hand, five aerobic days divided between swimming, biking, aerobic dancing, stair-climbing and distance running will stimulate the heart and lungs effectively and won't overload the support structures of the body. Again, when you are on a 12 month training regimen, it's critical to train as intelligently as possible.

7 SPECIFIC CONDTIONING: ANAEROBIC

The game of basketball consists of short-term, high intensity movements. Therefore, training your energy systems and musculature in a similar, anaerobic fashion is the best and most specific way to prepare yourself for the physiological demands of the sport. Perhaps the most common method of conditioning specifically for the game of basketball is to perform some sprints on the court at the end of practice. Unfortunately, many players view this as a form of punishment rather than a form of conditioning. For this reason, this all-important anaerobic activity is done somewhat begrudgingly and rather un-enthusiastically.

Even though court sprints are quite beneficial, there are other anaerobic conditioning methods that have a greater scientific basis and, therefore, are more precise and more productive. Indeed, different types of sprints will effect your body in varying ways. Furthermore, there's a certain progression of sprint training that is most desirable for stimulating improvement. A progressive system of anaerobic conditioning places a constant overload on your body, which will help you to become a basketball player who is as highly conditioned as possible.

ANAEROBIC PARAMETERS

In order for training to be considered "anaerobic," there are certain physiological guidelines that must followed. For example, your body works anaerobically during activities that last from one second to roughly three minutes – provided that your intensity of effort is great enough to elicit an anaerobic response. Anaerobic intensity can be measured the same way as aerobic intensity by monitoring your exercise heart rate. Exercising at a level of about 85 to 100 percent of your maximum heart rate will guarantee that the work is anaerobic. At high levels of intensity, your heart rate will not allow you to train much more than about three minutes. Remember, anaerobic training is characterized by high-intensity efforts done over brief periods of time. Unlike aerobic conditioning – where decreased training intensity can be sacrificed for increased training time – anaerobic conditioning must be performed as hard as possible.

Your anaerobic norms are related to the time and distance of the activity. If a three minute threshold is used as the maximum anaerobic time limit, a range of distances can be easily determined. In three minutes, most athletes can complete at least 880 yards and a few might even reach as much as 1320 yards.

The game of basketball consists of short-term, high-intensity movements such as jumping for a rebound or layup.

On the other end of the time continuum, your anaerobic system can be stressed effectively by all-out sprinting that lasts as little as five seconds per rep – which would cover about 30 to 40 yards.

WORK:REST RATIOS

Once running distances have been prescribed, the next step is to determine a rest (or recovery) interval. The duration of the recovery period is related to the distance of the sprint and the time that it takes to complete it. The rest interval is usually expressed in relation to the work interval. This is known as the "work:rest ratio" and is most often designated as 1:1, 1:2 or 1:3. These ratios state that an athlete will rest either one, two or three times the duration that takes to perform the sprint. As a general rule, the shorter the sprint time – and the higher the intensity – the greater the work:rest ratio. Because of the high level of intensity, any sprint of less than 30 seconds requires a 1:3 work:rest ratio. As an example, a twenty second sprint should receive a rest interval of about 60 seconds. Sprints from 30 to 90 seconds have between a 1:3 and 1:2 work:rest ratio. Finally, sprints from 90 to 180 seconds need between a 1:2 and 1:1 work:rest ratio. A summary of times, distances and work:rest ratios is shown below.

Summary of Times, Distances, and Work:Rest Ratios.

Work/Time (sec)	Distance (yds)	Work:Rest Ratio
0-30	0-220	1:3
30-90	220-660	1:3 to 1:2
90-180	660-1320	1:2 to 1:1

Note: The time ranges apply to both the highly and poorly conditioned.

METHODS OF ANAEROBIC TRAINING

There are several different methods for training anaerobically. In fact, any method that is used aerobically can also be used anaerobically. However, time and heart rate (i.e. intensity) parameters must be met in order for your training to be anaerobically-effective. For instance, pedaling all-out against a heavy resistance or swimming laps as fast as possible will develop your anaerobic pathways.

Perhaps the best anaerobic option of conditioning for basketball is to run. Since basketball is a running game, running would seem to be the most specific conditioning modality. You might be in excellent condition to ride a bike but not to run. Indeed, the carryover from running is more specific to basketball than any other conditioning modality. As such, most of the discussion about anaerobic conditioning will focus on running.

Interval Training

Interval training is a series of repeated bouts of exercise (e.g. sprints) alternated with periods of relief. This particular type of conditioning allows you to train harder and longer than continuous exercise at the same intensity. This is because rest intervals are systematically placed throughout the workout to permit partial recovery and a physiological comeback. So, with an appropriate amount of recovery between sprints, you can run a series of four 440 yard sprints at a pace that would cripple you after two or three consecutive 440s without a recovery period.

Your interval training program should be designed to promote an intended response. As a basketball player, one of your biggest concerns is your ability to run as hard as you can, recover quickly and sprint again with an all-out effort. Your anaerobic systems have a wide range of training time – anywhere from 1 to 180 seconds. A completely conditioned player will be able to run hard at both ends of this spectrum. As the season approaches, your workouts should become more specialized so that most of your individual sprints last less than about 15 seconds. This is most specific to the sport and most beneficial to your basketball conditioning.

An interval running program consists of seven different components which can be manipulated to produce an anaerobic overload. All seven of these elements are dependent upon an athlete's level of conditioning – a poorly conditioned athlete will not be able to perform as much work as a more highly conditioned athlete. These variables are:

1. The number of sprint repetitions.

This refers to the number of work intervals – or reps – to be performed, such as three reps of a prescribed distance.

2. The training distance.

The training distance is the high-intensity work effort. An example is a 100 yard run in a specified time. During a workout, sprint distances should begin with longer distance anaerobic running (880 and up) and taper down to shorter, more basketball-specific sprints (220 and below). As the season nears, distances of 100 yards and less should receive the most emphasis.

3. The work interval.

The work interval relates to the prescribed time of the sprint, such as running a specified distance in 30 seconds.

4. The recovery interval.

This is the prescribed time between sprints. For instance, the period between sprints might provide 90 seconds of recovery.

5. The work:rest ratio.

The work:rest ratio pertains to the relationship between the work interval and the recovery interval, such as 1:3, 1:2 and 1:1. As noted earlier, the rest period between sprints is related to the time and distance that is run and the intensity of effort – the shorter the time or distance and the higher the intensity, the greater the work:rest ratio.

6. The total workout distance.

The sum of all sprint distances performed in a workout is the total workout distance. With longer and middle distance sprints, the total workout distance should not exceed about 2 to 2 ½ miles (or 3520 to 4400 yards).

7. The number of weekly sprint workouts.

This refers to how often sprint training is done per week. The number of weekly sprint workouts depends upon the distances that are completed. Middle and long distance anaerobic running (440 and up) can be done 2 - 4 days per week; short distance sprints can be performed 3 - 5 workouts per week.

An interval running workout can be written in shorthand, such as 10 x 100 yds (0:13/0:39). This indicates that an athlete is to run ten 100 yard sprints and that each sprint should be run in 13 seconds with a rest interval of 39 seconds between each of the ten sprints. (Note that the work:rest ratio is 1:3 because each sprint is less than 30 seconds duration.)

The following is a detailed example of a six-week interval running program that is specific to the anaerobic nature of basketball.

Sample Six–Week Internal Running Program

Week	Sprint Reps	Distance (yds)	Work:Rest Ratio	Work Time	Rest Time	Workout Distance	Workouts per Week
1	3	880	1:1	2:30	2:30	3960	3
	2	660	1:2	1:50	3:40		
	2	880	1:1	2:25	2:25		
2	1	660	1:2	1:50	3:40	4180	3
	4	440	1:2	1:15	2:30		
	1	880	1:1	2:25	2:25		
3	1	660	1:2	1:45	3:30	4180	3
	4	440	1:2	1:15	2:30		
	4	220	1:3	0:35	1:45		
	1	660	1:2	1:40	3:20		
4	4	440	1:2	1:10	2:20	4100	4
	4	220	1:3	0:35	1:45		
	8	100	1:3	0:15	0:45		
	1	440	1:2	1:05	2:10		
	8	220	1:3	0:30	1:30		
5	10	100	1:3	0:15	0:45	4000	4
	10	50	1:3	0:07	0:21		
	10	30	1:3	0:04	0:12		
	10	220	1:3	0:30	1:30		
	10	100	1:3	0:14	0:42		
6	10	50	1:3	0:07	0:21	4100	4
	10	30	1:3	0:04	0:12		
	10	10	1:3	0:02	0:06		

Fartlek Training

Fartlek training is thought to be the predecessor of interval training and was originally developed by the Swedes. The Swedes are famous in physical education circles for developing systems of training that were basic in structure and used the outdoors as much as possible. As such, fartlek training was initially intended to be performed over natural terrain with courses that ranged from flat to steady inclines. For this reason, fartlek training really was a precursor to the hill training that is used by modern track athletes.

Sometimes referred to as "speed play," fartlek training is quite similar to interval training. In structure, fartlek training is informal and uses combinations of walking, jogging and running to achieve a training response. The work and relief intervals are left entirely up to the runner – you can change your pace and rest at your own discretion. Although your body's aerobic system would benefit from this method of conditioning, your anaerobic capacities can also be developed effectively. A sample fartlek workout that emphasizes your anaerobic system might look as follows:

1. Jog 440 yards

2. Walk 220 yards

3. Alternate sprinting 220 yards and walking 220 yards for ten minutes.

4. Walk 440 yards

5. Alternate sprinting 100 yards uphill and walking 100 yards downhill for six minutes.

6. Walk 440 yards

7. Alternate sprinting 50 yards and walking 50 yards for three minutes.

Acceleration Sprints

This system of anaerobic training has been used predominantly by the track community and those who are looking to increase their running speed. As the name implies, acceleration sprints are characterized by a gradual increase in running speed until a full, all-out sprint is reached. For example, an individual would begin by jogging, then increase to striding and finally accelerate to sprinting the prescribed distance. Recovery can consist of either easy jogging or walking between bouts of exercise. Increasing your speed gradually throughout the sprint allows you to concentrate on your running technique and stride length – two factors that are important to speed development. Acceleration sprints also provide a smooth transition towards full sprinting form, thereby minimizing any potential muscle strain or pull. A series of 100 yard acceleration sprints might look like this:

1. Jog 20 yards, stride 30 yards and sprint 50 yards
2. Walk 50 yards and repeat ten times

Sprint Training

The biggest difference between sprint training and the other types of anaerobic activities is the level of intensity. During pure sprint training, each sprint rep is done at full speed. Because maximum effort is required, the rest interval between sprints must be sufficient to permit maximum recovery. This type of training is as sport-specific as you can get since actual distances and times can be assigned to your sprints that are based upon the requirements of your sport. Pure sprint training should be used during pre-season and in-season conditioning because it is the best method for stimulating anaerobic improvement.

SKILL IMPROVEMENT -VS- CONDITIONING

When integrating skill work with conditioning activities, improvement in one area is usually sacrificed for improvement in the other. For instance, sprinting as fast as possible is anaerobic conditioning; dribbling a basketball is sport-specific skill work. If the two are combined – that is, sprinting as fast possible while dribbling a basketball – maximum improvement probably won't occur in either sprinting or dribbling. If your goal is to refine a skill such as dribbling, then that component needs to be addressed specifically with skill drills. Likewise, if your aim is to enhance your anaerobic abilities, then you must focus on that particular area with conditioning drills. Otherwise, technique is sacrificed for conditioning or conditioning is surrendered in order to perfect a skill. There's a very fine line here because your skill work and conditioning are blended together during a game and these two elements must be as game-realistic as possible. However, developing speed to perform particular skills is something different than anaerobic conditioning. Indeed, skill training and conditioning development are two different aspects of your training. As such, each component must be treated separately so that maximum benefits can be attained in both areas.

The conditioning of your anaerobic system is critical to your success as a basketball player. This system is also the most difficult to condition because your effort levels must always be at or near maximum. Through the use of the different methods of training described earlier, you'll be able to improve your anaerobic ability while providing enough variety in your program to prevent overtraining and burnout. As long as your training is systematic and progressive, you'll obtain maximum results.

Developing speed to perform a certain skill – such as dribbling a basketball – is different than anaerobic conditioning and must be addressed separately through skill drills.

8 CONDITIONING DRILLS: THE "DEADLY DOZEN"

Your capacity to train intensely throughout the year is a function of your ability to stay motivated towards your particular goals. Much of that motivation lies in the design of your training program. Variety in training allows you to keep your enthusiasm high because boredom is kept at a minimum. Variety also allows you to train your body in different planes and angles to prepare you for the game of basketball. One of the values of conditioning drills is that they provide variety along with the specificity needed for basketball.

The intent of this chapter is to describe twelve basic conditioning drills for the game of basketball. Over the years, the "Deadly Dozen" has had many different names. In fact, because of their degree of difficulty, some of these drills have received nicknames that are downright obscene!

Each of the twelve conditioning drills list several training variables, including the suggested number of reps, work (or exercise) interval, performance goal and recovery interval between repetitions. Brief descriptions and notes on making the drill more productive are also given for each drill.

It should be noted that the variables will differ depending upon the age, gender and conditioning level of the athlete. Another factor is whether the athletes perform the drills after practice in a pre-fatigued condition. The combination of reps, work interval, performance goal and recovery interval that are suggested in this chapter permit about 15 minutes of intermittent anaerobic activity per drill. The drills involve running forward, back pedaling, lateral movement, changes of direction and transitions between movements. The following symbols are used to designate the different types of movement and equipment:

Key to Diagrams			
⟶	running forward	=	eraser
/\/\/\/\▶	back pedaling	◦	cone
- - - - - - - ▶	lateral slide step		

The slide step and drop step are used during several drills. The slide step is a movement in which you shuffle laterally in a bent-knee position. Your center of gravity should be low and over the balls of your feet. When you slide step, don't bring your feet completely together – take a half step with each foot. Keep your head up, your back straight and your shoulders parallel to the direction of movement. The drop step is a fundamental technique in which you pivot on one foot and "drop" the other foot behind you, thereby making a half turn. This "opens" your hips and allows you to continue your slide in a different direction.

These dozen drills are just the tip of the iceberg as far as what is available. The variety of drills is endless and limited only by your imagination. As you become a better ball handler, you may add a ball to just about any of the drills. However, never sacrifice anaerobic conditioning for the sake of adding a dribbling dimension to a drill. The primary goal of conditioning drills is to get in shape to play basketball. Although times and performance goals are given, you should try to improve against your previous showing in each drill.

FOUR CORNER RUN

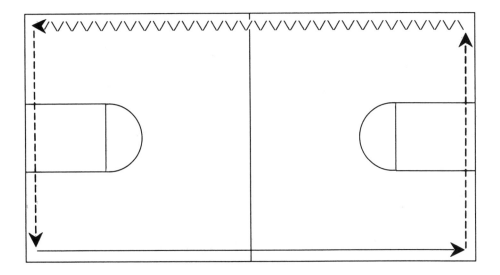

Suggested reps: 8

Work interval: Perform the drill in the shortest time possible

Performance goal: 35 seconds or less

Recovery interval: 90 seconds

Description: Starting in one corner of the court, sprint to the opposite baseline, slide step across that baseline to the corner, backpedal to the starting baseline and finish by slide stepping across the starting baseline.

Notes: The drill involves transitions between forward movement, slide stepping and backpedaling. The transition between these movements should be smooth but quick. Don't cross your feet when slide stepping. You should be facing downcourt throughout the entire drill.

60-SECOND "WIDTH" SPRINT

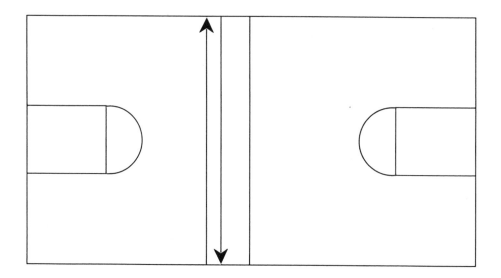

Suggested reps: 5

Work interval: 60 seconds

Performance goal: Cross the entire width of the court as many times as possible in one minute. Highly conditioned players can do this as many as 17 times in that period.

Recovery interval: 150 seconds

Description: Starting on one side line, sprint to the opposite side line, touch the line with your foot, turn and sprint back to the starting side line. Continue the drill for the prescribed amount of time.

Notes: Forward running, start-stop-start transitions and changes of direction are incorporated into this exercise. At the end of each sprint, you must touch the line with your foot, turn and sprint to the next line. This drill is similar to a "30-Second Suicide" except that it is performed across the width of the court instead of the length.

30-SECOND "SUICIDE"

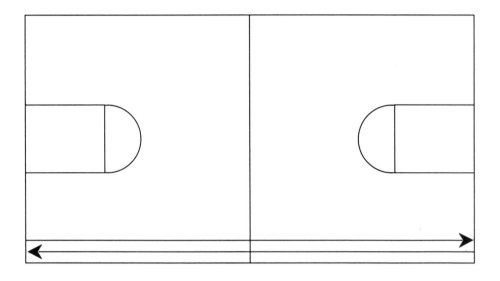

Suggested reps: 8

Work interval: 30 seconds

Performance goal: Cross the entire length of the court as many times as possible in 30 seconds. Highly conditioned players can do this as many as 6 times in that period.

Recovery interval: 90 seconds

Description: Starting on one baseline, sprint to the opposite baseline, touch the line with your foot, turn and sprint back to the starting baseline. Continue the drill for the prescribed amount of time.

Notes: Forward running, start-stop-start transitions and changes of direction are incorporated into this exercise. At the end of each sprint, you must touch the line with your foot, turn and sprint to the next line. This drill is similar to a "60-Second Width Sprint" except that it is performed across the length of the court instead of the width.

"SUICIDE" RUN

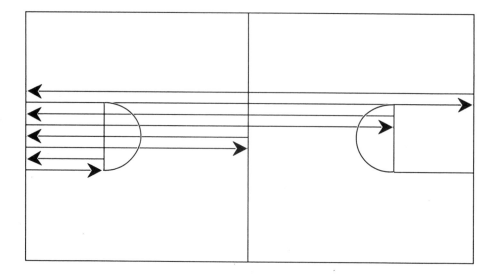

Suggested reps: 8

Work interval: Perform the drill in the shortest time possible

Performance goal: 32 seconds or less

Recovery interval: 90 seconds

Description: Starting on one baseline, sprint to the near free throw line and back, to half court and back, to the far free throw line and back and finally to the far baseline and back.

Notes: This drill involves forward running, start-stop-start transitions and changes of direction. At the end of each sprint, you must touch the line with your foot, turn and sprint to the next line.

BALL ROLL AND SLIDE

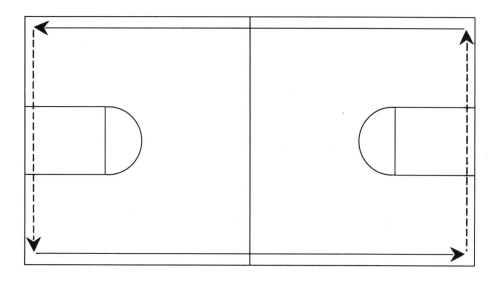

Suggested reps: 5

Work interval: 3 minutes

Performance Goal: Complete the drill as many times as possible in three minutes. Highly conditioned athletes can do this as many as 4 times in that period.

Recovery interval: 3 minutes

Description: Starting in one corner of the court, assume a crouched position with a basketball in your dominant hand. Roll the ball and tap it under control to the opposite baseline. At the opposite baseline, pick up the ball and hold it in your hands. Slide step across that baseline to the corner. At the corner, turn quickly to face the starting baseline. Repeat the ball roll, tap and slide across the starting baseline to the starting corner. Turn quickly and continue the drill for the prescribed amount of time.

Notes: This drill involves quick hands and a transition between forward movement and slide stepping. The ball roll and tap must be done quickly while keeping the ball under control. Maintain a bent-knee position with your head up and your chest over your knees. Don't cross your feet when slide stepping.

TRIANGLE SLIDE

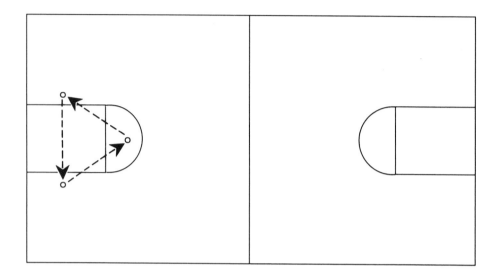

Suggested reps: 5

Work interval: 60 seconds

Performance goal: Complete as many "triangles" as possible in one minute. Highly conditioned players can do this as many as 8 times in that period.

Recovery interval: 150 seconds

Description: Three cones are needed for this drill. One cone should be placed three feet beyond the middle of the free throw line. The other two cones should be placed three feet beyond the middle of each lane line. Starting at the cone above the free throw line and facing mid-court, drop step and slide laterally to either of the mid-post cones. Drop step and slide laterally to the other mid-post cone. Drop step and slide laterally to the starting cone to complete the triangle. Continue the drill for the prescribed amount of time.

Notes: This drill incorporates lateral movement, drop steps and changes of direction. Keep your body in a low, bent-knee position with your head up and your back straight. Don't cross your feet when slide stepping. You should always be facing away from the center of the triangle throughout this drill. The initial direction of movement can be alternated each time the drill is done or each time a triangle is competed.

SPRINT SLIDE

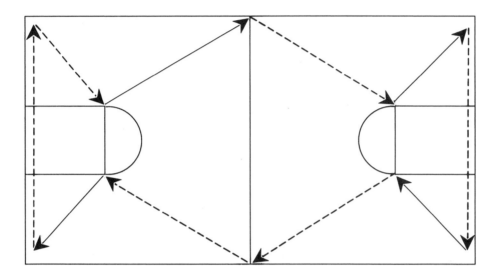

Suggested reps: 5

Work interval: Perform the drill in the shortest time possible

Performance goal: 50 seconds or less

Recovery interval: 135 seconds

Description: Starting in one corner of the court, slide step to the near corner of the lane line and free throw line, sprint to the near corner of the side line and midcourt, slide step to the near corner of the lane line and free throw line, sprint to the near corner of the court, slide step across that baseline to the next corner of the court, sprint to the near corner of the lane line and free throw line, slide step to the near corner of the side line and midcourt, slide step to the near corner of the lane line and free throw line, sprint to the near corner of the court, slide step across that baseline to the starting corner.

Notes: This drill incorporates forward running, slide stepping, changes of direction and transitions between movements. Don't cross your feet when slide stepping. For variety, you can alternate the directions that you are facing when slide stepping.

Z SLIDE

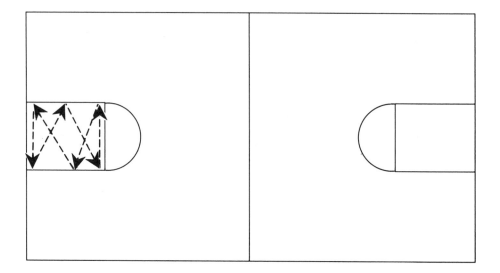

Suggested reps: 8

Work interval: Perform the drill in the shortest time possible

Performance goal: 30 seconds or less

Recovery interval: 90 seconds

Description: Starting in one corner of the lane line and free throw line, slide step diagonally across the lane to the middle of the lane line, drop step and slide diagonally across the lane to the corner of the lane line and baseline, drop step and slide across the baseline to the other corner of the lane line and baseline, pivot forward and slide step diagonally across the lane to the middle of the lane line, pivot forward and slide step diagonally across the lane to the corner of the lane line and free throw line, pivot forward and slide step across the free throw line to the starting corner.

Notes: Drop steps, pivots, lateral movement and changes of direction are involved in this drill. Keep your body in a low, bent-knee position with your head up and your back straight. Don't cross your feet when slide stepping.

BLOCK SLIDE

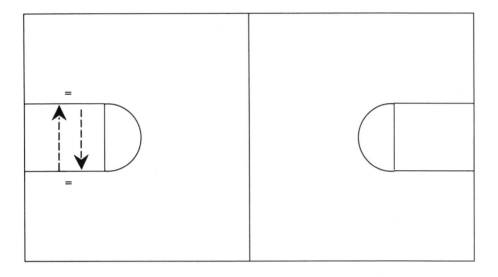

Suggested reps: 5

Work interval: 60 seconds

Performance goal: Slide step across the width of the lane as many times as possible in one minute. Highly conditioned players can do this as many as 20 times in that period.

Recovery interval: 150 seconds

Description: Three blackboard erasers are needed for this drill. One eraser should be placed on each side of the court one foot beyond the middle of the lane line. Hold the third eraser in the hand that is away from the middle of the lane. Starting at the middle of one lane line (standing inside the lane), slide step laterally across the lane to the opposite lane line. Switch the eraser on the floor with the eraser in your hand. Slide step back across the lane to the starting lane line and switch the erasers again. Continue the drill for the prescribed amount of time.

Notes: This drill involves lateral movement and hand speed. Keep your body in a low, bent-knee position with your head up and your back straight. Concentrate on short, quick movements. Don't cross your feet when slide stepping. Keep the eraser in the hand that is opposite the direction of movement (e.g. in your right hand when slide stepping to the left.)

BACKBOARD SLAP

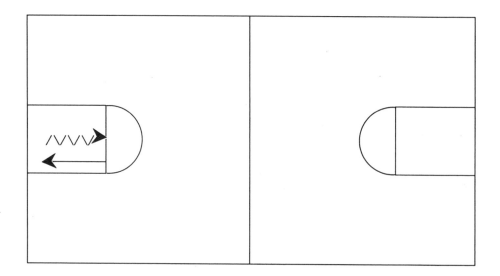

Suggested reps: 5

Work interval: 60 seconds

Performance goal: Cross the length of the lane to the basket, slap the backboard and return to the free throw line as many times as possible in one minute. Highly conditioned players can do this as many as 30 times in that period.

Recovery interval: 150 seconds

Description: Starting from behind the free throw line, run to the basket, jump up and slap the backboard with both of your hands. After landing, backpedal to the starting position. Continue the drill for the prescribed amount of time.

Notes: This drill incorporates forward running, jumping, start-stop-start transitions and backpedaling. You can lower the backboard if it is too high. If that's not possible, you can hang a piece of cloth or rope from it and slap that instead. As your vertical jump and lower body strength increases, you can gradually raise the height of the backboard or decrease the length of the cloth or rope.

COMBO

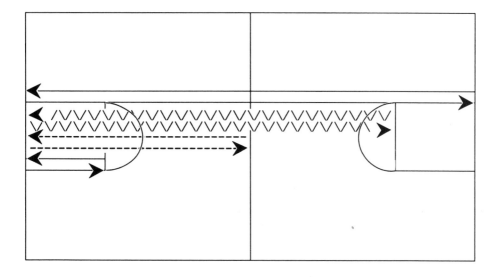

Suggested reps: 5

Work interval: Perform the drill in the shortest time possible

Performance goal: 50 seconds or less

Recovery interval: 135 seconds

Description: Starting on one baseline, sprint to the near free throw line and back, slide step to midcourt and back, backpedal to the far free throw line and back and finally sprint to the opposite baseline and back.

Notes: This drill involves forward running, slide stepping, backpedaling, start-stop-start transitions and changes of direction. At the end of each sprint, you must touch the line with your foot, turn and move quickly to the next line. This drill is similar to a "Suicide Run" except that it incorporates different types of movements.

35 SECOND "OPPOSITE HAND" LAYUP

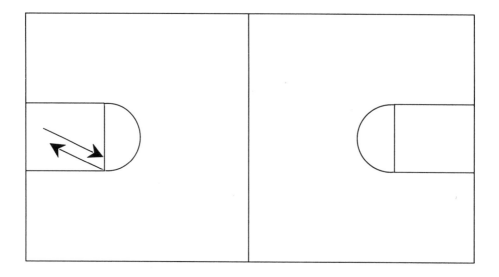

Suggested reps: 8

Work interval: 35 seconds

Performance goal: Cross the lane diagonally from one corner of the free throw line to the basket and perform as many "opposite hand" layups as possible in one minute. Highly conditioned players can do this as many as 6 times in that period.

Recovery interval: 90 seconds

Description: This drill requires a basketball. Your "opposite hand" is your nondominant or least-preferred hand. Starting from beyond one corner of the free throw line, dribble diagonally across the lane and lay the ball up with your opposite hand. Dribble back to the starting position. Continue the drill for the prescribed amount of time.

Notes: Forward movement, dribbling and jumping are involved in this exercise. All dribbling and shooting should be done with your least-preferred hand. However, if you're having trouble with this drill, you can use your dominant hand until your skills improve. This drill should only be performed when your ball handling and layup skills have progressed to the point where dribbling does not limit the intended conditioning effect.

OVERTIME:

MAXIMIZING YOUR RESULTS

9 NUTRITIONAL OVERVIEW: EATING TO WIN

Your nutritional habits are another factor that influence your performance potential. Unfortunately, this aspect of total conditioning is often overlooked and seldom addressed. Nutrition is the process by which food is selected, consumed, digested, absorbed and utilized by the body. This plays a critical role in your capacity to perform in the present and recover for the future. Truly, your ability to fully recuperate after an exhaustive activity directly effects your future performance and subsequent intensity in your strength training, conditioning activities and basketball competitions.

You can improve your nutritional "skills" by understanding the food sources, recommended intakes and physiological contributions of the various nutrients. It's also meaningful to examine your caloric "needs" along with the principles and procedures for gaining or losing weight in a desirable manner. Finally, a knowledge of what foods to eat before and after vigorous activity is helpful in maximizing your potential.

THE NUTRIENTS

Everything you do requires energy. Energy is measured in calories and is obtained through the foods – or nutrients – that you eat. Essentially, the foods that you consume serve as a fuel for your body. Food is also necessary for the growth, maintenance and repair of your body tissue (such as muscle and bone).

The foods that you eat are composed of six nutrients: carbohydrates, proteins, fats, water, vitamins and minerals. These six main constituents of food are divided into the macronutrients and the micronutrients. In order to be considered "nutritious," your food intake must contain the recommended percentages of the macronutrients as well as appropriate levels of the micronutrients. No single foodstuff satisfies this requirement. As such, variety is the key to a well-balanced diet.

The Macronutrients

As the name implies, macronutrients are needed in relatively large amounts. Three macronutrients – carbohydrates, proteins and fats – provide you with a supply of energy. Although it has no calories, water is also considered a macronutrient because it is needed in considerable quantities.

Carbohydrates

Carbohydrates – or "carbs" – are chemical compounds consisting of various combinations of carbon, hydrogen and oxygen molecules. The primary job of carbohydrates is to supply energy – especially during intense exercise.

Carbs are found in sugars (such as table sugar and honey), starches (like the starch in bread) and fibers. Carbohydrate-rich foods include potatoes, cereals, pancakes, breads, spaghetti, macaroni, rice, grains, fruits and vegetables.

Your body breaks down carbohydrates into glucose. As mentioned in an earlier chapter, glucose can be used as immediate energy during exercise or stored as glycogen in your liver and muscles for future use. Highly-conditioned muscles can stockpile as much as 50 percent more glycogen than poorly-conditioned muscles! When your glycogen stores are depleted, you feel over-whelmingly exhausted. For this reason, greater glycogen stores provide you with a physiological advantage. Therefore, your diet should be carbohydrate-based. In fact, at least 60 percent of your food intake should be in the form of carbohydrates. The minimum intake of carbohydrates should be at least four servings per day.

Proteins

Protein is necessary for the repair, maintenance and growth of biological tissue – particularly muscle tissue. In addition, protein regulates water balance and transports other nutrients. Protein is also an energy source in the event that adequate carbohydrates aren't available. Good sources of protein are beef, pork, fish, chicken, eggs, liver, dried beans and dairy products.

When proteins are ingested as foods, they are broken down into their basic "building blocks": amino acids. Of the 22 known amino acids, your body can manufacture 13 of them. The other 9, however, must be provided in your diet and are termed "essential amino acids." When a food contains all of the essential amino acids it is called a "complete protein." All animal proteins — with the exception of gelatin – are complete proteins. The protein found in vegetables and other sources is "incomplete protein" because it doesn't include all the essential amino acids.

The need for megadoses of protein by those who engage in rigorous physical activity has been drastically exaggerated and overrated. Skillful promoters of nutritional supplements have bestowed protein and amino acids with almost supernatural virtues, having the ability to do practically everything imaginable — even cure cancer! Protein is critical to your daily existence, but it doesn't promote any superhuman powers. Furthermore, any excessive dietary protein is either filtered through your kidneys or stored as fat. In short, there are no significant nutritional benefits obtained from the intake of additional protein. Approximately 20 percent of your food intake should be protein. You should consume two or three servings of protein-rich foods per day.

Protein is necessary for the repair, maintenance and growth of muscle tissue, but there is no need for megadoses of that particular nutrient.

Fats

It's hard to believe, but fats are essential to a balanced diet. First of all, fats serve as a concentrated source of energy during low level activities like sleeping or reading. This nutrient also helps you to absorb certain vitamins. Lastly, fats add considerable flavor to foods. (This makes food more appetizing — and also explains why fats are craved so much.)

Foods high in fat are butter, cheese, margarine, meat, nuts, milk products and cooking oils. Animal fats (such as butter, lard and fats in meats) are usually termed "saturated" and contribute to heart disease; vegetable fats (such as corn oil and peanut oil) are generally "unsaturated" and less harmful.

Fat is the only nutrient that remains basically in the same general state throughout the entire digestive process. There's really no need to add extra "fatty" food to your diet in order to get adequate fat. The fact is that most people consume far too much fat. Indeed, fats often accompany your carbohydrate and protein choices. In addition, foods are frequently prepared in such a way that fat is never difficult to obtain. For example, a baked potato is a great source of carbohydrates. However, when a potato is made into french fries, you'll get plenty of fat calories instead. Because of this, fat should be the first thing that is reduced in your diet. At most, 20 percent of your diet should be composed of fats. Unfortunately, the quantity of fat consumed by the average American typically exceeds this level – sometimes by twice the recommendation.

Finally, it should be noted that carbohydrates and proteins are converted to fat if not utilized by the body. Any fats that aren't used as energy are also stored as fats.

Water

Although water doesn't have any calories or provide you with energy, it is sometimes classified as a macronutrient because it is needed in rather large quantities. In fact, almost two-thirds of your bodyweight is water! Water lubricates your joints and regulates your body temperature. Water also carries nutrients to your cells and waste products away from your cells.

The best sources of water are milk, fruit juices and, of course, water. You should drink about one quart of water for every 1,000 calories you expend. (Caloric consumption will be discussed shortly.)

The Micronutrients

Vitamins and minerals are classified as micronutrients because they are needed in rather small amounts. Neither of these nutrients supplies any calories or energy. However, they do have many other important functions.

Vitamins and minerals – like proteins – have always been thought to have magical powers. The typical person lives by the attitude that if one pill is good, then more must be better. It's true that a deficit of vitamins and minerals can make you unhealthy, but consuming more than you need doesn't necessarily make you any healthier.

Vitamins

Vitamins are potent compounds that are required in very small quantities. As noted, these substances are not a source of energy but perform many different roles. For instance, Vitamin A helps you to maintain your vision at night and Vitamin C is necessary for wounds to heal. Vitamins occur in a wide variety of foods, especially fruits and vegetables.

Vitamins can be classified as either fat-soluble (vitamins A, D, E and K) or water soluble (vitamins B and C). Fat-soluble vitamins require proper amounts of fat to be present before digestion and absorption can take place. Consumption of excessive amounts of fat-soluble vitamins can produce toxic symptoms. Water soluble vitamins are found in foods which are naturally high in water content. Water-soluble vitamins are not stored in the body – excess amounts are simply passed through your system.

Minerals

Minerals are found in tiny amounts in foods. Nearly all the minerals that you need can be obtained with an ordinary intake of foods. Calcium, phosphorus, magnesium, potassium, iron and zinc are among the 21 essential minerals that must be provided by your food intake. Minerals have many functions, such as building strong bones and teeth, helping your muscles work and even enabling your heart to beat. Like vitamins, an adequate mineral intake can be obtained from a balanced diet that contains a variety of foods.

CALORIC CONTRIBUTIONS

It's necessary to understand that carbohydrates, proteins and fats provide different amounts of calories – or "cals." Carbohydrates and proteins yield 4 cals per gram. Fats are the most concentrated form of energy, containing 9 cals per gram. (Alcohol has 7 cals per gram.) From this information, you can determine the caloric contributions of each macronutrient in any food. For example, suppose a nutrition label notes that a certain food has 144 calories per serving and that each serving has 16 grams of carbohydrate, 2 grams of protein and 8 grams of fat. To find the number of calories that are supplied by each macronutrient, simply multiply their quantity of grams per serving by their energy yield. This information is summarized in the following chart.

Example of Caloric Content Based Upon the Energy Yield of the Macronutrients.

Macronutrient	Amount (g)	Energy Yield (cals/g)	Calories
Carbohydrate	16	4	64
Protein	2	4	8
Fat	8	9	72
		TOTAL CALORIES:	144

Note that even though this food has twice as many grams of carbohydrates as fats, exactly 50 percent of the calories (72 of the 144 calories) are furnished by fats. Incidentally, this food is actually a popular snack food – potato chips.

ESTIMATING CALORIC NEEDS

An individual's need for calories – or energy – is determined by several factors including age, gender, body condition, body composition, metabolic rate and activity level. Your caloric needs can be determined precisely by both direct and indirect calorimetry. However, these methods can be costly and impractical for most people. For a quick, reasonably accurate estimate of your daily energy needs, the U. S. Department of Agriculture suggests multiplying your body-weight in pounds by a factor that is determined by your level of activity. For females, the value is 18 if you're moderately active and 22 if you're very active; for males, the factors are 21 and 26. As an example, a 202 pound male who is very active requires about 5,252 calories per day to meet his energy needs [202 × 26 = 5,252].

Once you know how many calories you need, your next step is to determine how many of these calories should come from carbohydrates, proteins and fats. The chart on the following page shows a range of daily caloric consumptions from 1,500 to 6,000 calories per day in 250 calorie increments. The chart also lists the recommended intake of grams and calories for each of the three energy-providing nutrients. Simply locate your caloric needs in the far left-hand column and then read across that line to find the suggested daily amount of each nutrient. Using the previous example, someone who requires about 5,250 cals should consume around 788 grams of carbohydrates (3,150 cals), 263 grams of proteins (1,050 cals) and 117 grams of fat (1,050 cals). It should be noted that these numbers are based upon a diet that consists of 60% carbohydrates, 20% proteins and 20% fats.

Recommended Intake of Calories and Grams for Each of the Three Energy-Providing Nutrients, Based Upon Daily Caloric Consumption.

	Carbohydrates 60%		Proteins 20%		Fats 20%	
Cals/day	cals	g	cals	g	cals	g
1500	900	225	300	75	300	33
1750	1050	263	350	88	350	39
2000	1200	300	400	100	400	44
2250	1350	338	450	113	450	50
2500	1500	375	500	125	500	56
2750	1650	413	550	138	550	61
3000	1800	450	600	150	600	67
3250	1950	488	650	163	650	72
3500	2100	525	700	175	700	78
3750	2250	563	750	188	750	83
4000	2400	600	800	200	800	89
4250	2550	638	850	213	850	94
4500	2700	675	900	225	900	100
4750	2850	713	950	238	950	106
5000	3000	750	1000	250	1000	111
5250	3150	788	1050	263	1050	117
5500	3300	825	1100	275	1100	122
5750	3450	863	1150	288	1150	128
6000	3600	900	1200	300	1200	133

WEIGHT GAIN OR LOSS

Gaining, losing or maintaining weight is simply a matter of arithmetic. If you take in more calories than you use up, you'll have a "positive caloric balance" and gain weight; if you use up more calories than you consume, you'll be in a "negative caloric balance" and lose weight; lastly, if you take in the same amount of calories that you use up, you'll have a "caloric balance" and your weight won't change. However, a closer inspection of gaining and losing weight is necessary.

Gaining Weight

The potential to gain weight is determined by several factors, the most important of which is your genetic make-up. If your ancestors are tall and thin, then the odds are you'll look like that as well. This doesn't mean that you cannot gain weight. However, if you're 6′8″ and 180 pounds, don't expect to increase your weight to 240 pounds in one year!

In order to gain weight, you must consume more calories than you expend. The ultimate goal during weight gain is to increase your lean body mass. There's about 2500 calories in one pound of muscle. Therefore, if you consume 500 calories per day above your caloric needs (i.e. a +500 caloric "profit"), it will take you 5 days to add one pound of lean, fat-free weight. [500 cals/day X 5 days = 2500 cals]. So, if you need 5000 calories per day to maintain your bodyweight, you'll have to consume 5500 calories per day. It should be noted that your daily caloric profit should not be more than about 1000 - 1500 calories above your normal caloric intake. If your weight gain is more than about two pounds per week, it's likely that some excess calories will be stored in the form of fat. However, if your weight gain is less than about two pounds per week and is the result of a demanding strength training program in conjunction with a well-balanced nutritional intake, then it will probably be in the form of muscle tissue.

Proper weight gain relies upon total nutritional dedication for 7 days a week. Additional calories must be consumed daily on a regular basis until your desired weight gain is achieved. Science also suggests that your body absorbs food best when it is divided into several regular-sized meals intermingled with a few snacks. One or two large meals aren't absorbed by the body as well – most of these calories are simply jammed through your digestive system. In fact, if a large number of calories is consumed at one time, some calories will be diverted to fat deposits because of the sudden demand on your metabolic pathways. This has been referred to as "nutrient overload." A sample high-calorie – and high-carbohydrate – diet appears on the following page.

Example of a High-Calorie Diet (5,250 calories)

Meal	Selection	Calories
Breakfast	2 sups of bran flakes with raisins	290
	3 plain pancakes	180
	2 slices of white bread	110
	1 tablespoon of strawberry jam	55
	1 cup of orange juice	110
	1 cup of 1% low fat milk	100
Snack #1	1 bagel	165
	1 large orange	65
	1 large banana	100
Lunch	1 serving of bluefish (6 ounces)	270
	6 scallops	175
	1 large baked potato	145
	1 serving of white rice (½ cup)	90
	1 serving of ice cream (½ cup)	135
	1 cup of canned pears	195
	2 cups of 1% low fat milk	200
Snack #2	1 vanilla milkshake (11 ounces)	350
	1 large apple	125
Dinner	2 cups of minestrone soup	210
	1 chicken breast (2 halves)	320
	1 cup of white rice	180
	2 hard rolls	310
	1 cup of creamstyle corn	210
	1 cup of hot macaroni	155
	1 slice of apple pie	345
	1 cup of grape juice	165
Snack #3	1 peanut butter sandwich	300
	2 twisted Dutch pretzels	120
	1 glass of ginger ale (8 ounces)	75

Losing Weight

At one time or another, almost everyone has felt the need to lose weight. The need for weight loss should be determined by body composition rather than bodyweight – especially if you're an athlete. In general, athletes are larger and more muscular than the rest of the population. For instance, suppose two people were 6 feet tall and weighed 200 pounds. You might think that they were both overweight. However, what if one person had 20% body fat and the other person had 10% body fat? If this were the case, then only one person needed to lose weight – the one with the higher percentage of body fat. As such, the most reliable determinant for weight loss is your percentage of body fat. This can be measured in a variety of ways, although using skinfold calipers is generally considered to be the most practical method of assessment. Normal body fats for athletes are lower than the average population, ranging from about 12-22 percent for females and 5-13 percent for males.

You must expend more calories than you consume in order to lose weight. The primary goal of a weight loss program is to decrease your body fat. One pound of fat has about 3500 calories. As such, if you expend 500 calories per day below your caloric needs (i.e. a -500 caloric "deficit"), you'll lose one pound of fat in 7 days [700 cals/day × 500 cals = 3500 cals]. In this instance, if you need 5000 calories per day to maintain your bodyweight, you'll have to consume 4500 calories per day. In addition to reducing your caloric intake, a caloric deficit can also be achieved by increasing your energy expenditure – such as through additional aerobic activity. In fact, proper weight loss should be a combination of dieting and exercise.

Once again, the amount of weight loss will determine whether the caloric expenditure actually came from fat or muscle. If you lose more than about 2 pounds per week, it's likely that some of this weight reduction will be the result of lost muscle tissue and/or water.

Weight loss must be a carefully planned activity. Skipping meals – or all-out starvation – isn't a desirable procedure of weight loss, since you still need fuel for your athletic lifestyle. Oddly enough, losing weight should be done in a fashion similar to gaining weight. Frequent – but smaller – meals spread out over the day will suppress your appetite. Drinking plenty of water will give you a feeling of fullness without any calories.

THE PRE-GAME MEAL

A pre-game meal should accomplish several things, such as removing your hunger pains, fueling your body for the upcoming game and settling you psychologically. No foods will lead directly to a great performance when consumed several hours before a game. However, certain foods should be avoided prior to competition or exercise. For example, fats and meats are digested slowly. This means that the traditional steak dinner might actually be the worst possible meal to eat before a game! Other foods to omit include those that are greasy, highly seasoned and flatulent (gas-forming), along with any specific foods that you may personally find distressful to your system. If anything, your pre-game meal choices should be almost bland, yet appetizing enough so that you want to eat it.

Consumption of large amounts of sugar or sweets – like candy -- less than one hour before activity or competition should also be avoided. Sugar consumption causes a sharp increase in your blood glucose levels. Your body will respond to this by increasing its blood insulin levels to maintain a stable internal environment. As a result of this chemical balancing, your blood glucose is sharply reduced leading to hypoglycemia (low blood sugar), which decreases the availability of blood glucose as a fuel and causes a feeling of severe fatigue.

The best foods to consume prior to a game or exercise are carbohydrates. Carbs are easily digested and help maintain your blood glucose levels. Water is perhaps the best liquid to drink before competing. The amount of fluid intake should guarantee optimal hydration during the game.

The timing of your pre-game meal is also crucial. To ensure that the digestive process doesn't impair your performance, your pre-game meal should be eaten three hours or more before game time. In short, your pre-game meal should include foods that are familiar and well-tolerated – preferably carbohydrates.

RECOVERY FLUIDS/FOODS

After intense exercise or competition, proper nutrition will accelerate recovery and better prepare you for your next bout of work. Plenty of fluids should always be consumed to maintain acceptable hydration levels. If possible, drink a fluid that contains carbohydrates. Some commercial exercise beverages are high in carbohydrates, but read the label to be sure.

Ideally, you should try to ingest ½ gram of carbohydrates for every pound that you weigh within two hours of completing an intense workout. This should be repeated again within the next two hours. For instance, if you weigh 200 pounds, you'll need to consume about 100 grams of carbs (or 400 carbohydrate calories) within two hours after exercising and another 100 grams of carbs during the next two hours [½ × 200 = 100 grams].

MAGIC PILLS AND POTIONS

Athletes are constantly searching for safe and lawful ways to obtain a competitive edge. For this reason, numerous athletes give no second thought to spending huge sums of money on nutritional "supplements" that claim to improve athletic performance "legally" or "naturally." Food for thought: some compounds obtained from "nutrition" stores or mail-order companies are not subject to inspection by the Food and Drug Administration (FDA). Therefore, the exact content of such compounds is unknown and may not be represented accurately on the list of ingredients. Some products may contain small amounts of banned substances such as testosterone or other anabolic steroids or may actually be anabolic steroids but not labeled as such. Several of these supposed nutritional supplements have also been found to have such items as sawdust and chalk as part of their ingredients!

Fraudulent Claims

Many of these nutritional products don't support the performance-enhancement claims of the manufacturers. One of the most infamous nutritional supplements has a highly-appealing name meant to attract the emotions of the competitive consumer: Anabolic Mega-Pak. Unfortunately, a better description might be "Soy Bean Powder." Several years ago, the makers of Anabolic Mega-Pak came under heavy scrutiny by the Federal Trade Commission for "engaging in deceptive acts and practices" and "disseminating false advertisements." In other words, what was claimed to be in the product wasn't really in there and what it was supposed to do didn't really result.

That's just one example. Other companies have made claims about their products by taking research out of context, claiming university testing that didn't really occur, implying or falsely stating endorsement by professional groups and falsely claiming they were involved in research (or had "secret research results"). Worthless research references are regularly used to influence the consumer – often unpublished research from Eastern Europe – which is outdated, taken out of context and/or not peer-reviewed. Nowadays, there's a statement at the very bottom of many ads for supplements – usually in tiny print – that reads, "As with all supplements, use of this product will not promote faster or greater muscular gains. This product is, however, a nutritious low-fat food supplement which, like other foods, provides nutritional support for weight training athletes."

Smart Choices

Proper nutrition is critical in order to compete at the highest levels possible. The harder you train, the smarter you have to be in fueling your body. Good nutritional habits rely upon you making wise choices for 24 hours a day and 7 days a week. Once these choices become habits, your training will be that much easier and smarter.

If you are consuming a variety of foods that provide adequate calories and nutrients, there's no need for supplements. Research has concluded that nutritional supplements have little or no positive influence on performance and may even be physiologically damaging. Yet, the FDA once estimated that 18 million Americans are "bilked" of at least 2 billion dollars each year by nutritional supplements, special food products, book vendors and special devices reputed to solve nutritional ills. If you took the money used to purchase these expensive supplements and invested it in high-quality foods and snacks instead, you'd be much more successful in maximizing your potential. Remember, there are no shortcuts to proper nutrition.

10 FLEXIBILITY: S-T-R-E-T-C-H-I-N-G IT OUT

The easiest task to perform is sometimes the most difficult one to actually do. Perhaps the reason for this is that easy tasks are simple and, therefore, often taken for granted. Flexibility movements are undoubtedly the simplest and most effortless physical assignment for you to perform – the exertion level is low and relaxation is an absolute requirement. Nevertheless, ask any coach about flexibility training and most will agree that stretching is one of the hardest things to get athletes to do on their own.

Flexibility is defined as the range of motion that a joint can move through. It is a necessary component of total conditioning. Increasing your flexibility will allow you to do several things. First of all, you'll be less susceptible to injury. Secondly, you'll be able to exert your strength through a greater range of motion when you perform your basketball skills. Finally, stretching your muscles is a way of relieving and/or preventing general muscle soreness.

FLEXIBILITY PARAMETERS

Your flexibility is effected by several inherited characteristics, particularly your muscle-to-fat ratio and the insertion points of your muscles. In addition, your range of motion has structural limitations such as bones, tendons, ligaments and skin. It should be noted that flexibility is joint-specific – a high degree of flexibility in one joint doesn't necessarily indicate high flexibility in other joints.

"WARMING UP"

For years, "warming up" was synonymous with stretching. However, warming up and stretching are two separate entities and must be treated as such. A warm-up should precede your flexibility training. Warm-up activities usually consist of light jogging or calisthenics. Regardless of the warm-up activity, the idea is to increase your blood circulation and body temperature. Breaking a light sweat during the warm-up indicates that your body temperature has been raised sufficiently and you're ready to begin stretching your muscles. By the way, there's no need to stretch or warm-up prior to strength training – provided that you're performing a relatively high number of repetitions and lifting the weight in a controlled manner.

SEVEN STRETCHING STRATEGIES

Like all other forms of exercise, stretching movements have certain guidelines that must be followed. Here's some strategies to make your stretching safe and effective.

1. **Stretch under control without bouncing, bobbing or jerking movements.** Bouncing during the stretch actually makes it more painful and increases your risk of tissue damage.

2. **Inhale and exhale normally during the stretch without holding your breath.** Holding your breath elevates your blood pressure which disrupts your balance and breathing mechanisms.

3. **Each stretch should be easy and pain-free.** Pain is an indication that you're stretching at or near your structural limits.

4. **Relax during the stretch.** Relaxing mentally and physically will allow you to stretch your muscles throughout a greater range of motion.

5. **Hold each stretch for 30 - 60 seconds.** As your program progresses, you should increase the duration of each stretch.

6. **Attempt to stretch a little bit farther than the last time.** Progressively increasing your range of motion will improve your flexibility.

7. **Flexibility work should be done on a regular basis.** Stretching should be done at least once a day, especially before a practice, game, conditioning session or any other activity that will involve explosive, ballistic movements.

FLEXIBILITY EXERCISES

The following pages describe ten flexibility movements. Each movement lists the muscle(s) stretched, a brief explanation and notes on making the exercise safer and more effective. There are many variations of these stretches that involve the same muscle groups. Feel free to use or include your own favorite stretches.

You only get out of stretching what you put into it. Applying the previously mentioned guidelines to the subsequent stretches will permit you to increase your current range of motion. Additionally, you'll be less likely to be injured and perform closer to your athletic potential.

STANDING FORWARD "V"

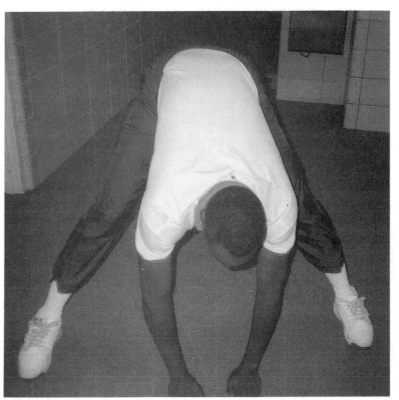

Muscles stretched: hips, hamstrings, calves, upper back, lower back

Description: From a standing position, place your feet slightly wider than shoulder width apart. Keeping your knees fairly straight, bend over at the waist and reach down as far as possible.

Notes: If possible, place your palms flat on the ground. Concentrate on keeping your knees fairly straight.

STANDING LATERAL "V"

Muscles stretched: hips, hamstrings, calves, upper back, obliques, lower back

Description: Starting from the same position as the "Standing Forward V", slowly rotate to one side of your body. Grasp your ankle and pull your head toward your leg. Repeat the stretch to the other side of your body.

Notes: Don't lift your torso up between stretches. There should be a slow, smooth transition when moving from one side of your body to the other.

GROIN STRETCH

Muscles stretched: hips, iliopsoas, hip adductors, hip abductors, hamstrings, calves

Description: Place your feet slightly wider than shoulder width apart. Without moving your feet, slowly shift your body to one side. Bend the knee on the side that you're moving toward and keep the other leg straight. To achieve a greater stretch, place one hand near your hip and push your straight leg downward.

Notes: There should be a slow, smooth transition when moving from one side of your body to the other.

"SAIGON" SQUAT

Muscles stretched: hips, hip adductors, hamstrings, calves

Description: Place your feet slightly wider than shoulder width apart. Keeping your head up and your torso fairly erect, slowly lower your hips to the floor. Reach down and place your hands on the floor.

Notes: Concentrate on keeping your hips down without bending forward significantly at the waist. Your heels should remain flat on the floor throughout the stretch.

KNEE PULL

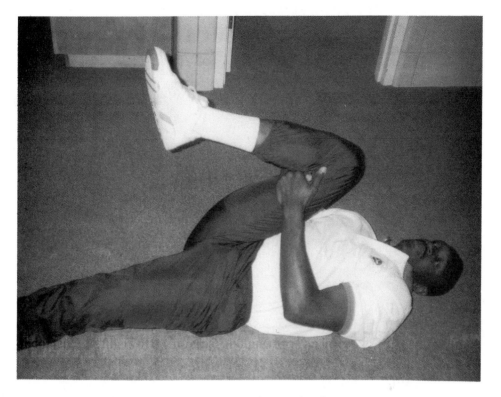

Muscles stretched: hips, hamstrings, lower back

Description: Lay supine on the floor with your legs extended. Grasp one leg behind the knee and pull it toward your chest. Keep your other leg straight. Repeat the stretch for the other side of your body.

Notes: Using your arms to pull your leg will allow you to obtain a better stretch.

CROSSOVER

Muscles stretched: hip abductors, hamstrings, obliques, lower back

Description: Lay supine on the floor with your legs extended. Keep your shoulders flat on the floor and move one leg across your body. Repeat the stretch for the other side of your body.

Notes: Keep your shoulders flat on the floor and your legs extended as you perform this stretch.

"QUAD" STRETCH

Muscles stretched: quadriceps, hip flexors, abdominals

Description: Lay prone on the floor with your legs extended. Reach back, grasp one ankle and pull your heel toward your hips. Repeat the stretch for the other side of your body.

Notes: Concentrate on pulling your heel as close to your hips as possible.

SHOOTER'S STRETCH

Muscles stretched: chest, upper back, shoulders, triceps

Description: From a standing position, reach behind your head and place your hand between your shoulder blades. Grasp the elbow of that arm with your other hand. Slowly pull that elbow behind your head. Repeat the stretch for the other side of your body.

Notes: As you pull your elbow, try to "walk" your hand farther down your spine.

STANDING CALF

Muscle stretched: calves

Description: Starting from a standing position, step forward with either foot. Bend your front knee forward but keep your back foot flat on the floor and your back leg straight. Repeat the stretch for your other leg.

Notes: The heel of your back foot should remain flat on the floor. Your chest should be over your front knee throughout this stretch.

WALL WALK

Muscles stretched: chest, upper back, shoulders, biceps

Description: Stand sideways as close to a wall as possible. Reach up as high as you can with the arm that is nearest the wall and place your palm flat against it. "Walk" your hand up the wall to stretch even farther. Repeat the stretch for the other side of your body.

Notes: Keep your feet flat on the floor and your shoulders square. Always try to reach up as high as possible.

11 TWENTY QUESTIONS . . . AND TWENTY ANSWERS

This book has described a comprehensive strength and conditioning package that will help you maximize your potential as a basketball player. However, there are a few more topics and issues in this area that must be addressed. Therefore, this chapter examines some of the most frequently asked questions from coaches and athletes.

1. Should I do high reps if I want to tone my muscles and low reps if I want to increase their size?

There's absolutely no conclusive evidence to suggest that low reps will bulk up your muscles and high reps will tone your muscles. If you are placed on the same strength program as someone else for several months (i.e. the same number of sets, reps and exercises) the odds are that the two of you won't develop the same way. That's because everyone inherits a different potential for increasing their size and strength. Some people are predisposed toward developing large, heavily-muscled physiques while others are predisposed more toward a defined physique. Then there are the lucky ones who have a genetic tendency for both muscular size and definition. Those are the guys and gals that you see posing in the glossy muscle mags. If all you had to do to develop huge muscles was to follow the program of the latest bodybuilding champ, then there would certainly be millions of men and women walking around who look like Mr. or Ms. America. But that's not the case. What you do have, however, is millions of guys and gals knocking themselves out by trying to follow the programs of the current physique stars. Whether you do a set of low reps, high reps or intermediate reps you're still going to develop according to your inherited characteristics – provided that the sets are done with similar levels of intensity. The next time you're in the weight room, take a look at various training partners. You'll see that people who work out together usually have different builds – despite training with the same number of sets, reps and exercises as each other. The fact is that you simply cannot change your genetic profile.

Finally, remember that you're a basketball player, not a bodybuilder. Using the repetition ranges noted earlier in the book (i.e. 10-15 for the hips, 8-12 for the legs and midsection and 6-10 for the upper torso) will allow you to develop your muscles in a safe, productive manner according to your genetic potential.

If you want to improve your jump shot, you've got to practice your jump shot in the same way that you might use it in a game.

2. What's the best way to improve my jump shot?

There are two requirements necessary for you to increase your efficiency at performing sports skills. First of all, you must literally practice the motor skill for thousands and thousands of task-specific repetitions. Each time you do the skill it must be done with perfect technique so that its specific movement pattern becomes firmly ingrained in your "motor memory." The skill must be practiced perfectly and exactly as you would use it in game situations. Remember, practice makes perfect ... but only if you practice perfect.

Secondly, you must strengthen the major muscle groups that are used during the performance of that skill. However, it should not be done in a manner that mimics a particular sports skill so as not to confuse or impair the intended movement pattern. A stronger muscle can produce more force; if you can produce more force, you'll require less effort and be able to perform the skill more quickly, more accurately and more efficiently. But again, this is provided that you've practiced enough in a correct manner so that you'll be more skillful in applying that force.

So, if you want to improve your jump shot, you've got to practice your jump shot in the same way that you might use it in a game (i.e. against a defender, off the dribble, etc.) and with regulation equipment (i.e. a regulation size basketball, a standard height basket, a regulation diameter hoop, etc.). Finally, you must strengthen the muscles used in a jump shot, namely your hips, legs, upper torso and arms.

Incidentally, if you happen to lift weights immediately before shooting a basketball it will upset or "throw off" your shot. However, the effect is only temporary – your shooting "touch" will return as soon as your neuromuscular pathways adjust to the fatigue. In other words, strength training won't ruin your shot.

3. I've heard that barbell squats are bad for your knees. What's the scoop?

Indeed, barbell squats create excessive shear forces in the knee joint. As the length of the legs increase, so does the shearing effect in the knee – someone with long legs is more prone to injury than someone with short legs. In addition, placing a barbell on your shoulders causes compression of your spinal column, which could result in a herniated or ruptured disc. In fact, research has revealed that when someone squats with as little as 1 to 1½ times bodyweight, the force in the low back region is actually 6 to 10 times bodyweight. That means if a 180 pound player does barbell squats with about 180 - 270 pounds, the load on the low back area can be anywhere from 1,040 - 1,800 pounds! The exact amount of force is a function of how far the weight is from your low back – an individual with a long torso subjects his or her low back to higher forces than someone with a shorter torso.

So, someone with a long torso and long legs is not only at a severe biomechanical disadvantage during a barbell squat, but also exposes the joints to undue forces and a higher risk of injury. Therefore, barbell squats are inappropriate and ill-advised for most people – especially those with the body proportions that are characteristic of most basketball players (i.e. elongated spines and legs). The same muscles used in a barbell squat – namely the hips, quads and hams – can be exercised in a safer manner with a movement such as a leg press.

4. I noticed that I'm starting to get a little "spare tire" around my midsection. Should I do lots of sit-ups to get rid of the fat?

No! That's a common misconception that pertains to the localized loss of body fat or, in exercise physiology parlance, the myth of "spot reducing." It isn't necessary to perform thousands – or even hundreds – of repetitions in order to exercise your abdominals. Yet, many people perform countless repetitions of sit-ups, knee-ups and other abdominal exercises every day with the belief that this will give them a highly prized set of "washboard abs" Although such Olympian efforts will certainly work your underlying abdominal muscles, it has little effect on your overlying fatty tissue. The reason you can't lose fat in one area alone is that when you exercise, you are drawing upon energy stores from all over your body as a source of fuel – not just from one specific area. So, you can do sit-ups until you pass out, but that won't automatically trim your midsection! Quite simply, spot reduction is impossible.

Your abs should be treated like any other muscle group. Once an activity for the abs exceeds about 70 seconds in duration, it becomes a test of endurance rather than strength. You can work your abdominals effectively in a time efficient manner by exercising them to the point of concentric muscular failure between 8-12 reps (or about 40 - 70 seconds).

5. I'm a female basketball player. Won't lifting weights make me less flexible and bulk me up?

A properly conducted strength training program will not reduce your flexibility – provided that you exercise throughout a full range of movement. If you still have fears about losing flexibility, then you should perform a comprehensive stretching routine both before and after your strength program (see Chapter 10). These stretches can be the same ones that you do before a practice or game. If you prefer, you can also stretch your muscles immediately following each exercise.

A properly conducted strength training program will not reduce a woman's flexibility or cause her to develop large, unsightly muscles.

Gains in muscular strength are usually accompanied by an increase in the size of muscles. However, numerous studies have shown that the degree of muscular hypertrophy is much less pronounced in females. In fact, one estimate is that the number of women who have the genetic potential to significantly increase the size of her muscles is about one in a million!

There are several physiological reasons that prevent or minimize the possibility of a woman increasing the size of her muscles to a significant degree. First of all, most women are genetically bound by an unfavorable – and unchangeable – ratio of muscle to tendon (i.e. short muscle bellies coupled with long tendinous attachments).

In addition, compared to men most women have low levels of plasma testosterone. The low level of this growth-promoting hormone restricts the degree of muscular hypertrophy in women.

Another physiological factor is the fact that females tend to inherit higher percentages of body fat than males. For example, the average 18 to 22 year old female is about 22-26 percent body fat, whereas the average male of similar age is about 12-16 percent. This extra body fat tends to soften or mask the effects of weight training.

In short, it is physiologically improbable that a woman will develop large muscles that are unsightly or unfeminine. If you're wondering about female bodybuilders, they inherit a greater potential for muscular hypertrophy than the average woman. In addition, they often appear to be more muscular on stage than they actually are. Prior to a competition, they've restricted their caloric intake – often severely – thereby reducing their body fat and water. They've also "pumped up" their muscles backstage immediately before the competition. Finally, the stage lighting, their clothing and the oil rubbed on their bodies all contribute to the illusion.

6. Will plyometrics improve my vertical jump?

Not necessarily. The term plyometrics applies to any exercise or jumping drill which uses the myotatic or stretch reflex of a muscle. This particular reflex is elicited when a muscle is pre-stretched prior to a muscular contraction and results in a more powerful movement than would otherwise be possible. For example, just before you jump vertically – such as for a rebound – you bend at your hips and knees. This "countermovement" pre-stretches your hip and leg muscles allowing you to generate more force than if you tried to jump without first squatting down. Popular exercises based on this principle include bounding, hopping, and various box drills. Upper body plyometrics frequently incorporate medicine balls.

Within the past few years, a growing number of strength and fitness professionals have begun to question these drills in terms of being productive and safe. Why? First of all, there's been absolutely no scientific evidence that proves plyometrics are a productive form of exercise. Most of the support for plyometrics has been from personal narratives and sketchy research. One plyometric guru even admits that the information about plyometrics is anecdotal and "methodologically weak." More importantly, the possibility of injury from plyometrics is positively enormous. In fact, many prominent orthopaedic surgeons, physical therapists and athletic trainers view plyometrics as "an injury waiting to happen." When performing plyometrics, the musculoskeletal system is exposed to repetitive trauma and extreme biomechanical loading. Potential injuries include – but aren't limited to – sprained joints, muscle strains, heel bruises, shin splints, stress-related fractures, meniscal damage, patellar tendinitis, ruptured tendons and vertebral compression. Young athletes are especially vulnerable.

So, plyometric exercises have not been proven to be productive and carry an unreasonably high risk of injury. Your vertical jump can be improved by simply practicing your jumping skill and technique in the same manner that you would use it in a game and by strengthening your major muscle groups, especially your hips and legs.

7. What's the earliest age that someone can begin a strength training program?

Weight training exercises are usually inappropriate for children younger than the age of 13 or 14. In the case of prepubescents, calisthenic-type movements that involve their bodyweight as resistance (such as push-ups and sit-ups) are quite effective for building strength without placing an inordinate amount of stress on their bones and joints. When weight training is used by adolescents, the exercises should be throughout a full range of motion in a controlled manner. The repetitions should be relatively high – such as 15-20 for the lower body and 10-15 for the upper body. The movements should be performed 2-3 times per week on nonconsecutive days and involve their major muscle groups (hips, legs and upper torso).

8. Why can't a strength workout last more than one hour?

Your body prefers to use carbohydrates – stored as glycogen in your muscle and glucose in your liver and bloodstream – as its primary fuel during intense exercise. After about one hour of intense activity, your body exhausts these carbohydrate stores and goes after a secondary source of energy: proteins. The problem is that proteins are necessary for you to resynthesize muscle tissue. When you break down proteins for fuel, you're creating a situation much like that found in cases of starvation. For this reason, it's not a good idea to go beyond about one hour of intense exercise.

9. I know that it's important for my players to do strength training, conditioning and skill work. What order would I schedule these three activities on the same day?

For best results, skill work should be done first, followed by conditioning activities and then strength training. Of all three activities, the one that is most important to the sport is skill work. If your players are exhausted after running and lifting, they'll be spent both physically and mentally. Therefore, they won't practice very hard or work on their technique very well. In fact, they're sure to be inattentive and their performance will probably be quite careless, labored and awkward. Furthermore, players will be more prone to injury if they practice in a pre-fatigued state. Because of this, it's best not to practice skills after intense lifting or conditioning.

Since the sport of basketball has a greater endurance component, the conditioning activities should precede the strength workout. Research also indicates that better overall results are obtained when endurance work is performed before strength training.

10. Is it true that barbells will increase size and strength faster than machines?

You won't develop one way with machines and another way with barbells – assuming that your levels of intensity are similar with both modalities. Recall that a muscle must be fatigued with a workload in order to increase in size and strength. Since your muscles don't have a brain, eyeballs or cognitive ability, they can't possibly "know" the source of the workload. So, it doesn't matter whether you fatigue your muscles with a resistance that comes from a machine, a barbell, a cinder block or a human being. The sole factors in determining your response from strength training are your inherited characteristics and your level of intensity – not the equipment that you use.

Food for thought: The next time you watch a basketball game, see if you can tell which players lift with free weights, which players lift with machines and which players didn't lift themselves out of bed when it was time to strength train!

11. What exactly are steroids and are they really that dangerous?

Anabolic-androgenic steroids are synthetic derivatives of the male sex hormone testosterone. Its "anabolic" or growth-promoting effects include increased skeletal mass, nitrogen retention and protein synthesis. Steroids also have "androgenic" or masculinizing effects such as increased facial and body hair, a deepening of the voice and an increased libido.

Are they dangerous? You better believe it. In fact, University of Toledo Strength Coach Ken Mannie says, "The list of adverse effects [from steroid use] reads like a Stephen King horror story." Coach Mannie isn't exaggerating. Here's a partial list of the dangerous side effects that are documented in the medical literature:

For starters, there are mental side effects which may include psychiatric disorders, severe depression, manic depression, paranoia, grandiose delusions, visual and auditory hallucinations, irritability, a feeling of invincibility, extreme mood swings that can be borderline psychotic and an abnormally high level of unpredictable hostility and aggression (called 'roid rage.)

There are also numerous physical/physiological side effects which may consist of insomnia, increased cholesterol levels, high blood pressure, cancerous tumors, cardiovascular kidney dysfunction, acne (usually on the back), a loss of scalp hair, rectal bleeding, unprovoked nosebleeds and a predisposition to tendon and ligament injuries. (Apparently, connective tissue does not respond to steroids to the same degree that muscle tissue does. This creates a situation in which the connective tissue cannot keep up with the demands from using heavier weights. It's like putting an engine from a Mack truck into a Volkswagen!)

Using steroids also increases the possibility of liver cancer, blood pooling in the liver and jaundice (which gives the eyes and skin a yellowish tint). If you inject steroids into your body, you'll find that punctures, bruise marks, scar tissue and a callused butt are the least of your worries. Users also risk blood poisoning and the spread of communicable diseases – including AIDS – from contaminated needles as well as neural dysfunction due to improperly placed needles. Adolescents who use steroids may experience a pre-mature fusing of their epiphyseal growth plates that may stunt their growth.

There's also several gender-specific side effects as well. When a man starts to introduce extra testosterone into his body, then his body will reduce its own production in order to maintain a stable internal environment. If too much "foreign" testosterone is added, his body will no longer produce its own supply and the result is a feminizing effect. This chemical balancing results in testicular atrophy, a high-pitched voice and enlarged, female-like breasts. If this bit of hormonal irony isn't enough, males can also expect fluid retention (which gives the face and skin a bloated, puffy look), prostate enlargement, a decreased sperm count, functional impotency and an increased or decreased libido. Females may experience irreversible physical changes, including an enlargement of the clitoris, reduced breast size, uterine atrophy, a deepening of the voice, cessation of menstruation and increased facial and body hair. Women who use steroids also increase their risk of getting breast cancer and of bearing children with birth defects.

Most importantly of all, deaths have been directly – and legally – attributed to steroid use.

The most efficient program is one that produces the maximum possible results in the least amount of time.

It should also be noted that anabolic steroids are categorized as Class II drugs, which makes their use restricted in the same manner as barbiturates. Current legislation has penalties that includes a maximum $1,000 fine and a maximum one year sentence for possession as well as a $250,000 fine and up to 5 years in prison for distribution. It also gives federal drug enforcement officials the authority to seize assets and money earned through drug trafficking.

If you play around with steroids you're gambling with your physical and mental well-being, perhaps permanently. It's in your best interests to steer clear of this or any other "performance-enhancing" drug.

12. Wouldn't it be better to exercise my bodyparts on alternate days instead of doing all of them on one day?

You've described what's known as a "split routine." This has been a popular training method of bodybuilders and recreational lifters for many years. In this type of routine, you work out on consecutive days but exercise different muscles. For example, you might "split" your muscle groups such that you exercise your lower body on Mondays and Thursdays and your upper body on Tuesdays and Fridays.

It's certainly true that a person using a split routine doesn't usually exercise the same muscles two days in a row. Recall, however, that it takes a minimum of 48 hours in order for the body to replenish its stockpiles of carbohydrates (or glycogen) following an intense workout. So, if you worked out your lower body on Monday you depleted your body's carbohydrate stores. Even if you train different muscles on Tuesday you haven't had the necessary 48 hours to fully recover those stores.

There may be some individual variations in recovery ability but split routines are generally inappropriate, inefficient and unreasonable for the majority of the population. If you're like most people, time is a precious commodity. Because of this, you should emphasize the quality of work done in the weight room rather than the quantity of work. Don't forget, the most efficient program is one that produces the maximum possible results in the least amount of time.

13. Can you recommend a sport-specific conditioning test for basketball?

A conditioning test that is specific to basketball has an endless number of possibilities. However, the test should be designed to evaluate an individual's physical readiness to participate in the sport of basketball. Since basketball is a series of short-term anaerobic movements that are performed over a lengthy aerobic base, a legitimate conditioning test should address those two areas.

The first component of a basketball-specific conditioning test is an aerobic evaluation. Most fitness professionals generally agree that an activity must last a minimum of 12 minutes in order for aerobic benefits to occur. With this in mind, one method of assessing aerobic conditioning could be a 12 minute run on the track. The goal of this test is to see how far you can run in 12 minutes. A variation of this test would be a 2 mile run. In this case, the object is to see how fast you can run 2 miles.

An anaerobic evaluation is the second ingredient of a basketball-specific conditioning test. An athlete's ability to recover between bouts of anaerobic activity is also a factor that must be evaluated. Recall that anaerobic work occurs within a time frame of about one second to three minutes. As such, several of the conditioning drills described in Chapter 8 can be used to test anaerobic ability. The 60-Second "Width" Sprint, 30-Second "Suicide," and "Suicide" Run are particularly appropriate. As an example, suppose the Suicide Run is used as an anaerobic appraisal during the conditioning test. In this instance, the goal might be to run a series of eight "suicides" as fast as possible with 90 seconds of recovery between repetitions.

The aerobic and anaerobic segments of the test can be administered on the same day or on separate days. If the aerobic and anaerobic evaluations are performed on the same day, the recovery interval between the two should be about one-half the time that it took to complete the aerobic portion of the test. So, if a 2 mile run was completed in 12 minutes, a six minute recovery period is required before proceeding with the anaerobic evaluation. Finally, keep in mind that the performance goals of the test will differ depending upon the age, gender and conditioning level of your athletes.

14. I've heard that lifting weights explosively will increase my speed and quickness. Is that true?

No, it's not. To date, there's been no conclusive evidence in the literature to suggest that lifting weights at a high rate of speed converts your slow twitch (ST) fibers to fast twitch (FT) fibers. Furthermore, explosive lifting does not preferentially recruit your FT fibers. Muscle fibers are recruited in an orderly fashion according to the intensity or force requirements and not by the speed of movement. Demands of low muscular intensity are met by ST fibers. Intermediate fibers are recruited once the ST fibers are no longer able to continue the task. FT fibers are finally recruited only when the other fibers cannot meet the force requirements. All fibers are working when the FT fibers are being used. In short, movements performed in an explosive or ballistic manner do not bypass the ST and intermediate fibers in order to specifically recruit the FT fibers.

High-velocity movements are actually less productive than movements performed in a slow, deliberate manner. Here's why: Whenever you lift a weight explosively, momentum is introduced to provide movement to the weight or resistance. After the initial explosive movement, little or no resistance is encountered by the muscles throughout the remaining range of motion. In simple terms, the weight is practically moving under its own power. To illustrate the effects of momentum on muscular tension, imagine that you pushed a 100 pound cart across the length of the court at a deliberate, steady pace. In this instance, you maintained a constant tension on your muscles for the entire distance. Now, suppose that you were to push the cart across the court again. This time, however, you accelerated your pace to the point where you were running as fast as possible. If you were to stop pushing the cart at midcourt, it would continue to move by itself because you gave it momentum. So, in this case, your muscles had resistance over the first half of the court but not over the last half of the court. The same effect occurs in the weight room. When weights are lifted explosively, there is tension on the muscles over the initial part of the movement but not over the last part. In effect, the requirement for muscular force is reduced and so are the potential strength gains.

Explosive lifting can also be dangerous. Dr. Fred Allman, a past president of the American College of Sports Medicine, states, "It is even possible that many injuries ... may be the result of weakened connective tissue caused by explosive training in the weight room." Using momentum to lift a weight increases the internal forces encountered by a given joint; the faster a weight is lifted, the greater these forces are amplified – especially at the point of explosion. When the forces exceed the structural limits of a joint, an injury occurs in the muscles, bones or connective tissue. No one knows what the exact tensile strength of ligaments and tendons is at any given moment. The only way you can ascertain tensile strength is when the structural limits are surpassed. Then, of course, it's too late. Therefore, you must be concerned with an exercise's speed of movement because you simply don't know the structural limitations of your body's various connective tissues.

It's much safer and more efficient to raise the weight without any jerking or explosive movements and to lower it under control. Raising the weight in about 1-2 seconds and lowering it in about 3-4 seconds will ensure that the speed of movement is not ballistic in nature and that momentum does not play a significant role in the efficiency of the exercise.

15. How often should I max out?

Never! It's dangerous when you try to see how much weight you can lift for a one repetition maximum (1-RM). Attempting a 1-RM with heavy weights places an inordinate and unreasonable amount of stress on your muscles, bones and connective tissue. You'll get injured when this stress exceeds the structural integrity of those components. A 1-RM attempt also tends to increase blood pressure beyond that which is normally encountered when using submaximal weights. These concerns are magnified if you are a younger adolescent. Finally, a 1-RM lift is a highly specialized skill that requires a great deal of technique and practice. The repetition ranges suggested throughout the book will allow you to train more safely.

16. What exercises in the weight room are specific for basketball?

Your question raises a number of important issues. Are there sport-specific or even position-specific exercises? Should a basketball player perform different exercises than a football player or a swimmer? Or, should a power forward perform a strength workout that differs from that of a center or a shooting guard?

A basketball player has the same muscles which function in the same manner as any other athlete. For example, your bicep muscle flexes your lower arm around your elbow joint. The same is true for a diver, shot putter, quarterback, lacrosse player and defensive lineman. It follows that there is no such thing as a sport-specific or position-specific exercise. For that matter, there aren't any gender-specific exercises, either. Some athletes might perform certain movements as a precaution to prevent an injury to a joint that receives a lot of stress in their particular sport, such as a wrestler using neck exercises. Athletes might also perform a movement to focus on a particular muscle group that is absolutely critical to their sport. For instance, a golfer who relies on grip strength might exercise his or her forearms while a soccer player would not. Other than that, athletes should select movements that exercise their muscles in the safest and most efficient way possible – regardless of sport or activity. Remember, skill training and conditioning are specific to a sport but strength training is general.

Skill training and conditioning are specific to a sport but strength training is general.

17. I read somewhere that athletes should do power cleans because it's specific to sports movements and increases explosive power. What's a power clean?

A power clean is basically the initial phase of a competitive, Olympic-style lift known as the "clean and jerk." Power cleans have long been touted as being specific to an incredibly wide range of skills from the breast stroke to the golf swing to the shot put. It's absolutely impossible for one movement to be identical to such a broad group of differing skills. Indeed, how can something be specific to everything?

Using weighted implements to simulate or mimic sports skills has been thought to contribute to the learning of specific motor patterns. Individuals often practice with weighted objects -- such as barbells, dumbbells and medicine balls -- during this "overload training" with the expectation of improving performance. However, studies indicate that overload training is not accompanied by a measurable improvement in performance in the skills that have been practiced with weighted objects. The support for overload training is purely anecdotal.

If there were a correlation between weightlifting skills and other sports skills then highly successful weightlifters would excel at literally every sports-related movement that they attempted. So, if five members of the Bulgarian National Weightlifting Team were placed on a basketball court they should easily win every game! Naturally, this wouldn't happen. That's because there is absolutely no "carryover" between weightlifting skills and other athletic skills.

The Principle of Specificity is well-documented throughout motor learning literature. Briefly, it states that your activities must be specific to the intended skill in order for maximal improvement to occur. Specific means exact or identical. . . not similar or just like. So, power cleans may be similar to jumping for a rebound and an exercise like lunges may be just like driving toward the hoop but power cleans will only help you get better at doing power cleans and lunges will only help you get better at doing lunges. Likewise, tossing medicine balls around is great for improving your skill at tossing medicine balls around and nothing else. Furthermore, there is no exercise done in the weight room – with barbells or machines – that will expedite the learning of sports skills. One motor learning researcher has concluded that "any attempt to improve performance by utilizing objects that are slightly heavier than normal while practicing gross motor skills that will be later used in sports competition seems to be hardly worth the time spent and the money paid for the weighted objects."

In addition, a movement like a power clean is an extremely complex motor skill. Like any other motor skill, it takes a lot of time and patience to master its specific neuromuscular pattern. This valuable time and energy could be used more effectively elsewhere – such as perfecting your dribbling or shooting skills. More importantly, a power clean is inherently dangerous because it is performed explosively. Recall that ballistic movements are also inefficient due to the involvement of momentum. Finally, "explosive" lifting does not translate into "explosive" athletic skills. For these reasons, power cleans should only be done by competitive Olympic-style weightlifters – and only because it's part of their sport.

18. When I stop lifting weights my muscles will turn to fat, right?

Wrong! It's a common misconception that muscle can be changed into fat. In truth, you cannot change muscle into fat – or vice versa – any more than you can change lead into gold. Muscle tissue consists of special contractile proteins that allow movement to occur. The composition of muscle tissue is about 70% water, 22% protein and 7% fat. On the other hand, fatty tissue is composed of spherical cells that are specifically designed to store fat. Fatty tissue is about 22% water, 6% protein and 72% fat. Because muscle and fat are two different and distinct types of biological tissue, your muscles can't convert to fat when you stop lifting weights. Similarly, lifting weights – or doing any other rigorous activity – won't cause fat to change into muscle. The fact is that muscles atrophy – or become smaller – from prolonged disuse and muscles hypertrophy – or get larger – as a result of physical exercise.

19. I hear a lot about periodization. Isn't it the most effective way of gaining strength?

In recent years, there's been a lot of discussion about periodization or "cycling." Essentially, periodization is a theoretical training schedule popularized by weightlifters to peak for their competition. The idea is to change or "cycle" the number of sets, reps and workload of the exercises performed in the weight room. For example, in Week #1 you might do 3 sets of 10 reps in each exercise with 75 percent of your 1-RM; in week #2 you might do 4 sets of 8 reps with 80 percent of your 1-RM and so on, until you are performing a 1-RM.

Periodization has been adopted as a means of scheduling the strength training of athletes in sports other than competitive weightlifting. However, the concept of periodization is based upon the fact that highly competitive weightlifters peak for only several meets a year. What good is that for a basketball player who must peak two or three times a week for several months? Indeed, what games do you peak for? Aren't they all important? Imagine an athlete saying, "Sorry about my rebounding tonight, coach, but I'm not scheduled to peak for 10 more days."

The question you must ask yourself is, "Am I training to become a better basketball player or a better weightlifter?" Trying to implement periodization is not only confusing but also unnecessary. There's more efficient and far less complicated ways of addressing your strength training needs.

20. As a coach, I'm concerned about the progress of my athletes in the weight room. What strength tests can you recommend?

Strength testing isn't really necessary to monitor your athletes' progress. If your athletes are recording their workout data – and they should – you can simply check their workout cards to evaluate their strength levels. This doesn't mean that strength testing cannot be done – some coaches use it as a motivational tool. That's fine, as long as the strength test doesn't become a weightlifting meet.

The most popular – and traditional – way to assess muscular strength has been to determine how much weight an individual can lift for a one repetition maximum (1-RM). It's been noted earlier that attempting a 1-RM is potentially dangerous. So, how can muscular strength be measured in a safe and practical – yet reasonably accurate – manner without having someone max out? The answer lies in the relationship between strength and anaerobic endurance. There is a direct relationship between the percentage of maximal load (strength) and reps-to-fatigue (anaerobic endurance): As the percentage of maximal weight increases, the number of reps decreases in an almost linear fashion. Unless you have an injury or other musculoskeletal disorder, this kinship between your muscular strength and your anaerobic endurance remains constant. Since there is a distinct relationship between these two variables, you can determine anaerobic endurance by measuring strength, and you can also determine your strength by measuring anaerobic endurance.

This relationship is not exactly linear but close enough to determine a reasonably accurate linear approximation for describing the relationship between the two variables. In fact, the following mathematical equation can be used to predict a 1-RM based upon reps-to-fatigue:

$$\text{PREDICTED 1-RM} = \frac{\text{Weight Lifted}}{1.0278 - .0278X}$$

X = the number of reps performed

Example: Suppose that a male athlete did 8 reps-to-fatigue with 150 pounds. First, multiplying .0278 by the number of reps [8] equals .2224. Subtracting .2224 from 1.0278 leaves .8054. Dividing .8054 by the weight lifted [150 pounds] yields a predicted 1-RM of about 186 pounds.

In other words, he can do 8 reps with about 80.54 percent (or .8054) of his predicted 1-RM. Regardless of whether his strength increases or decreases, he will always be able to perform exactly 8 reps with roughly 80.54 percent of his maximum. Therefore, if he increases his 8-RM (his anaerobic endurance) by 20 percent [from 150 to 180 pounds] then he'll also increase his 1-RM (his muscular strength) by 20 percent [from 186 to 223 pounds].

It appears as if the relationship is not quite as linear beyond about 10 reps. So, this formula is only valid for predicting a 1-RM when the number of reps-to-fatigue is less than 10. It should also be noted that if the reps exceed about 10, then the test becomes less accurate for evaluating anaerobic endurance as well as for estimating a 1-RM. At any rate, a test of anaerobic endurance – though not a direct measure of pure maximal strength – is much safer than a 1-RM lift because it involves submaximal loads.

One final note: The purpose of strength testing should not be to compare the strength of one person to another. It's unfair to make strength comparisons between individuals because each person has a different genetic potential for achieving muscular strength. Strength testing is much more meaningful and fair when an individual's performance is compared to his or her last performance – not the performance of others.

12 YEAR-ROUND STRENGTH AND CONDITIONING CALENDAR

The previous 11 chapters have presented safe, efficient and productive information for the development of a strength and conditioning program. This final chapter contains a detailed description for scheduling your strength and conditioning activities throughout an entire year. This "Strength and Conditioning Calendar" will give you a basic idea of what activities to do and when to do them during different parts of the year. Since everyone's situation is different, much of the calendar is general. For specific information, please refer to the preceding chapters.

The calendar is divided into the three primary training seasons: Offseason (April - August), Preseason (September - October), and Inseason (November - March). The starting and ending dates of these seasons may vary according to your level of competition (i.e. high school, college, etc.). In general, however, the schedule will still be appropriate and useful.

The calendar includes the following activities and related areas:

1. **Strength Training.** The calendar details when strength training activities should be scheduled during the year.

2. **Aerobic Conditioning.** The suggested duration of aerobic training is listed in parentheses.

3. **Anaerobic Conditioning.** The recommended number of sprint reps and distances for anaerobic training is shown, such as 1 x 880, 1 x 660 and 4 x 440.

4. **Agility.** The number of conditioning drills to be selected from the "Deadly Dozen" is given in parentheses.

5. **Rest Period.** A brief "rest period" is integrated into the schedule prior to preseason training to avoid mental and physical exhaustion.

6. **R & R.** An extended rest period after the season – otherwise known as "Rest & Relaxation" – is also added.

7. **A fictitious schedule of competition.** Beginning in June, the calendar proceeds through an imaginary schedule of practices and games including a Preseason Tournament, a Conference Tournament, Playoffs and a Championship Tournament.

The recommendations on the calendar can be modified depending upon your age, gender and conditioning level. In addition, the method of conditioning will depend upon the equipment that is available (i.e. stationary bikes, treadmills, etc.).

THE FINAL INGREDIENT

This book contains the ingredients that are necessary for you to improve your strength and conditioning – except for one component. The last ingredient for this program to be successful is your dedication and desire to improve. The program must be followed religiously and regularly. The material in this book will help you to reach your athletic goals by decreasing your risk of injury and by improving your potential as a basketball player – but only if you take the information and apply it. The authors wish you strength and health in your pursuit of realizing your athletic potential.

June
Conditioning for Basketball

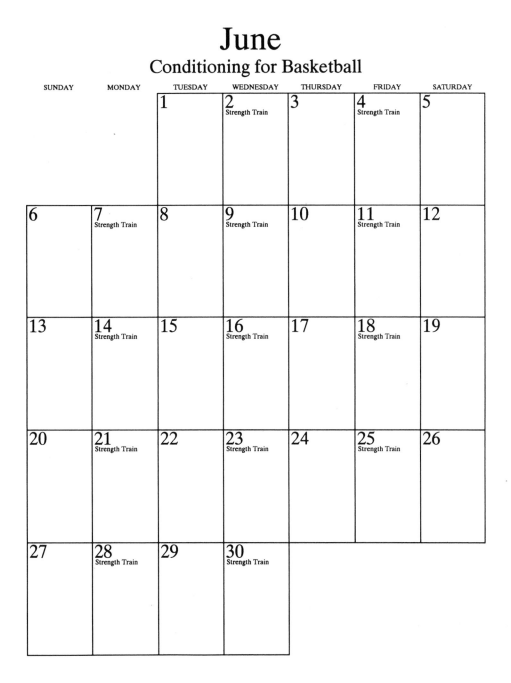

SUNDAY	MONDAY	TUESDAY	WEDNESDAY	THURSDAY	FRIDAY	SATURDAY
		1	2 Strength Train	3	4 Strength Train	5
6	7 Strength Train	8	9 Strength Train	10	11 Strength Train	12
13	14 Strength Train	15	16 Strength Train	17	18 Strength Train	19
20	21 Strength Train	22	23 Strength Train	24	25 Strength Train	26
27	28 Strength Train	29	30 Strength Train			

July
Conditioning for Basketball

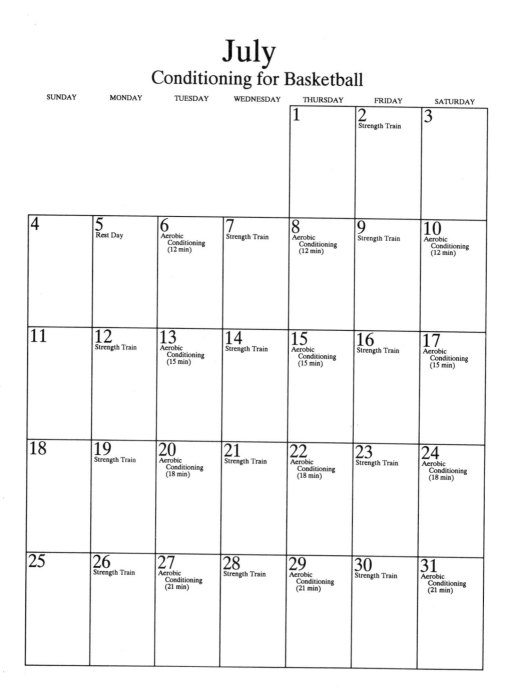

SUNDAY	MONDAY	TUESDAY	WEDNESDAY	THURSDAY	FRIDAY	SATURDAY
				1	2 Strength Train	3
4	5 Rest Day	6 Aerobic Conditioning (12 min)	7 Strength Train	8 Aerobic Conditioning (12 min)	9 Strength Train	10 Aerobic Conditioning (12 min)
11	12 Strength Train	13 Aerobic Conditioning (15 min)	14 Strength Train	15 Aerobic Conditioning (15 min)	16 Strength Train	17 Aerobic Conditioning (15 min)
18	19 Strength Train	20 Aerobic Conditioning (18 min)	21 Strength Train	22 Aerobic Conditioning (18 min)	23 Strength Train	24 Aerobic Conditioning (18 min)
25	26 Strength Train	27 Aerobic Conditioning (21 min)	28 Strength Train	29 Aerobic Conditioning (21 min)	30 Strength Train	31 Aerobic Conditioning (21 min)

August
Conditioning for Basketball

SUNDAY	MONDAY	TUESDAY	WEDNESDAY	THURSDAY	FRIDAY	SATURDAY
1	2 Strength Train	3 Aerobic Conditioning (21 min)	4 Strength Train	5 Aerobic Conditioning (21 min)	6 Strength Train	7 Aerobic Conditioning (21 min)
8	9 Strength Train	10 Aerobic Conditioning (24 min)	11 Strength Train	12 Aerobic Conditioning (24 min)	13 Strength Train	14 Aerobic Conditioning (24 min)
15	16 Strength Train	17 Aerobic Conditioning (27 min)	18 Strength Train	19 Aerobic Conditioning (27 min)	20 Strength Train	21 Aerobic Conditioning (27 min)
22	23 Strength Train	24 Aerobic Conditioning (30 min)	25 Strength Train	26 Aerobic Conditioning (30 min)	27 Strength Train	28 Aerobic Conditioning (30 min)
29	30 Strength Train	31 Aerobic Conditioning (30 min)				

September
Conditioning for Basketball

SUNDAY	MONDAY	TUESDAY	WEDNESDAY	THURSDAY	FRIDAY	SATURDAY
			1 Begin Rest Week	2	3	4
5	6	7 End Rest Week	8 Strength Train & Aerobic Conditioning (20 min)	9	10 Strength Train & Aerobic Conditioning (20 min)	11
12	13 Strength Train & Aerobic Conditioning (20 min)	14 Aerobic Conditioning (30 min)	15 Strength Train & Aerobic Conditioning (20 min)	16	17 Strength Train & Aerobic Conditioning (20 min)	18
19	20 Strength Train & Aerobic Conditioning (20 min)	21 Aerobic Conditioning (30 min)	22 Strength Train & Aerobic Conditioning (20 min)	23 Aerobic Conditioning (30 min)	24 Strength Train & Aerobic Conditioning (20 min)	25
26	27 Strength Train & 2x880, 1x660, 4x440	28	29 Strength Train	30		

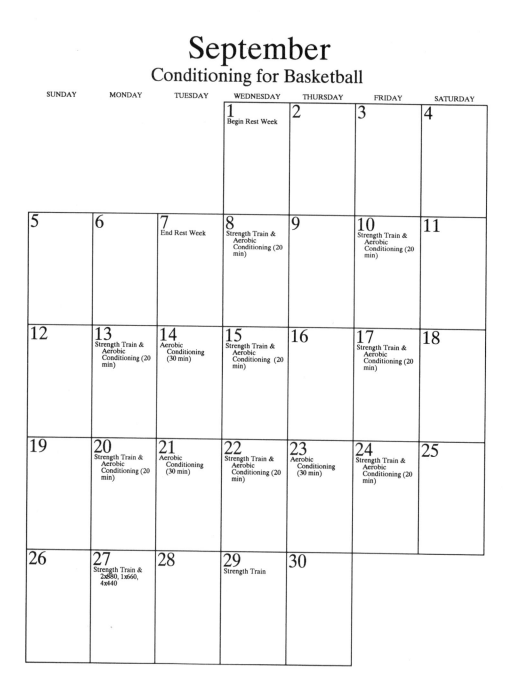

October
Conditioning for Basketball

SUNDAY	MONDAY	TUESDAY	WEDNESDAY	THURSDAY	FRIDAY	SATURDAY
					1 Strength Train & 2x880, 1x660, 4x440	**2**
3	**4** Strength Train & 1x880, 1x660, 4x440, 4x220	**5** Agility (2)	**6** Strength Train	**7** Agility (2)	**8** Strength Train & 1x880, 1x660, 4x440, 4x220	**9**
10	**11** Strength Train & 1x660, 4x440, 4x220, 8x100	**12** Agility (2)	**13** Strength Train	**14** Agility (2)	**15** Strength Train & 1x660, 4x440, 4x220, 8x100	**16**
17	**18** Strength Train & 1x440, 8x220, 10x100, 10x50, 10x30	**19** Agility (2)	**20** Strength Train	**21** Agility (2)	**22** Strength Train & 1x440, 8x220, 10x100, 10x50, 10x30	**23**
24	**25** Strength Train & 10x220, 10x100, 10x50, 10x30, 10x10	**26** Agility (2)	**27** Strength Train	**28** Agility (2)	**29** Strength Train & 10x220, 10x100, 10x50, 10x30, 10x10	**30**
31						

November
Conditioning for Basketball

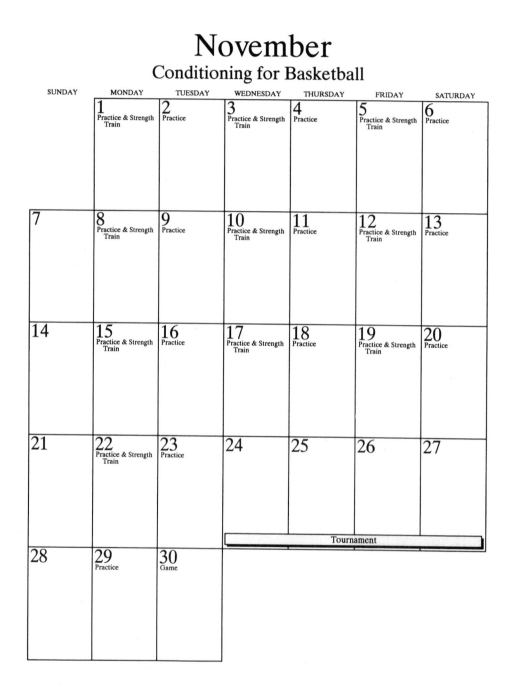

SUNDAY	MONDAY	TUESDAY	WEDNESDAY	THURSDAY	FRIDAY	SATURDAY
	1 Practice & Strength Train	2 Practice	3 Practice & Strength Train	4 Practice	5 Practice & Strength Train	6 Practice
7	8 Practice & Strength Train	9 Practice	10 Practice & Strength Train	11 Practice	12 Practice & Strength Train	13 Practice
14	15 Practice & Strength Train	16 Practice	17 Practice & Strength Train	18 Practice	19 Practice & Strength Train	20 Practice
21	22 Practice & Strength Train	23 Practice	24	25	26	27
			Tournament			
28	29 Practice	30 Game				

December
Conditioning for Basketball

SUNDAY	MONDAY	TUESDAY	WEDNESDAY	THURSDAY	FRIDAY	SATURDAY
			1 Practice	2 Practice & Strength Train	3 Practice	4 Game
5	6 Practice & Strength Train	7	8	9 Game	10 Practice	11 Game
			Practice			
12 Strength Train	13 Practice	14 Game	15 Practice & Strength Train	16	17	18 Game
					Practice	
19 Strength Train	20 Practice	21 Game	22 Practice	23 Game	24 Practice	25 Game
26 Strength Train	27 Practice	28 Game	29 Practice	30 Game	31 Practice	

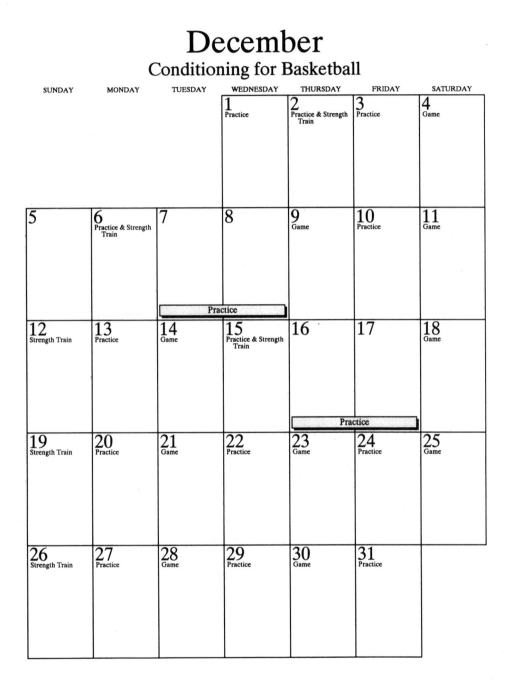

January
Conditioning for Basketball

SUNDAY	MONDAY	TUESDAY	WEDNESDAY	THURSDAY	FRIDAY	SATURDAY
						1 Rest Day
2 Strength Train	**3** Practice	**4** Game	**5** Practice	**6** Game	**7** Practice	**8** Game
9 Strength Train	**10** Practice	**11** Practice & Strength Train	**12** Practice	**13** Game	**14** Practice	**15** Game
16 Practice & Strength Train	**17** Practice	**18** Game	**19** Practice	**20** Game	**21** Practice	**22** Game
23 Practice & Strength Train	**24** Practice	**25** Practice & Strength Train	**26** Practice	**27** Game	**28** Practice	**29** Game
30 Practice & Strength Train	**31** Practice					

February
Conditioning for Basketball

SUNDAY	MONDAY	TUESDAY	WEDNESDAY	THURSDAY	FRIDAY	SATURDAY
		1 Game	2 Practice	3 Game	4 Practice	5 Game
6 Strength Train	7 Practice	8 Game	9 Practice	10 Game	11 Practice	12 Game
13 Strength Train	14 Practice	15 Practice & Strength Train	16 Practice	17 Game	18 Practice	19 Game
20 Strength Train	21 Practice	22 Practice & Strength Train	23 Practice	24 Game	25 Practice	26 Game
27 Strength Train	28 Practice					

March
Conditioning for Basketball

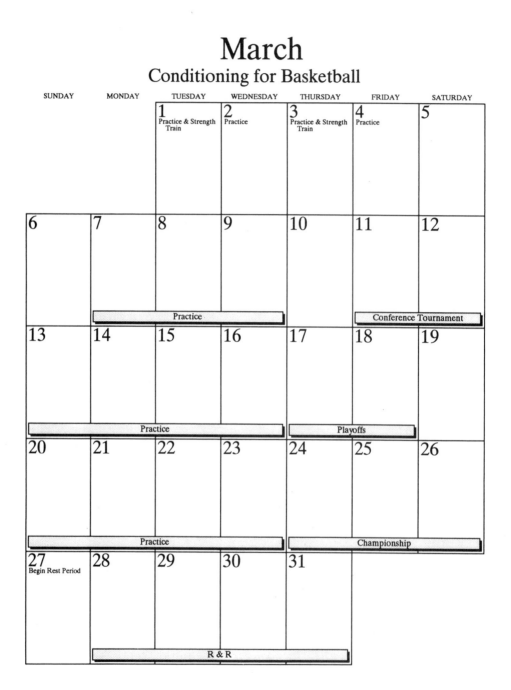

SUNDAY	MONDAY	TUESDAY	WEDNESDAY	THURSDAY	FRIDAY	SATURDAY
		1 Practice & Strength Train	**2** Practice	**3** Practice & Strength Train	**4** Practice	**5**
6	**7**	**8**	**9**	**10**	**11**	**12**
		Practice			Conference Tournament	
13	**14**	**15**	**16**	**17**	**18**	**19**
		Practice		Playoffs		
20	**21**	**22**	**23**	**24**	**25**	**26**
		Practice		Championship		
27 Begin Rest Period	**28**	**29**	**30**	**31**		
		R & R				

April
Conditioning for Basketball

SUNDAY	MONDAY	TUESDAY	WEDNESDAY	THURSDAY	FRIDAY	SATURDAY
					1	2
					R & R	
3	4	5	6	7	8	9
			R & R			
10	11	12	13	14	15	16
			R & R			
17 End Rest Period	18 Strength Train	19	20 Strength Train	21	22 Strength Train	23
24	25 Strength Train	26	27 Strength Train	28	29 Strength Train	30

May
Conditioning for Basketball

SUNDAY	MONDAY	TUESDAY	WEDNESDAY	THURSDAY	FRIDAY	SATURDAY
1	2 Strength Train	3	4 Strength Train	5	6 Strength Train	7
8	9 Strength Train	10	11 Strength Train	12	13 Strength Train	14
15	16 Strength Train	17	18 Strength Train	19	20 Strength Train	21
22	23 Strength Train	24	25 Strength Train	26	27 Strength Train	28
29	30 Strength Train	31				

BIBLIOGRAPHY

Brown, Shaun. *Providence Friars Strength & Conditioning Manual.* Providence, RI: Providence College, 1989.

Brzycki, Matt. *A Practical Approach to Strength Training.* 2d ed. Indianapolis, IN: Masters Press, 1991.

_____ . "Strength Testing: Predicting a One Rep Max From Reps-to-Fatigue." *The Journal of Physical Education, Recreation and Dance* 64, no. 1 (January 1993): 88-90.

_____ . "Strength Training an Injured Bodypart." *Scholastic Coach* 61, no. 10 (May/June 1992): 70-72.

_____ . "The Steroid Gamble: Do Ya Feel Lucky?" *Athletic Conditioning Quarterly* 1, no. 3 (May 1992): 3-4.

Cappozzo, Aurelio et al. "Lumbar Spine Loading During Half Squat Exercises." *Medicine and Science in Sports and Exercise* 17, no. 5 (October 1985): 613-20.

Clark, Nancy. *Nancy Clark's Sports Nutrition Guidebook.* Champaign, IL: Leisure Press, 1990.

Crouch, James E. *Functional Human Anatomy.* 3d ed. Philadelphia: Lea & Febiger, 1978.

Darden, Ellington. *The Nautilus Bodybuilding Book.* Chicago: Contemporary Books, 1982.

_____ . *The Nautilus Book.* Chicago: Contemporary Books, 1985.

_____ . *The Nautilus Nutrition Book.* Chicago: Contemporary Books, 1981.

Duda, Marty. "Elite Lifters at Risk for Spondylolysis." *The Physician and Sportsmedicine* 15, no. 10 (October 1987): 57-59.

_____ . "Plyometrics: A Legitimate Form of Power Training?" *The Physician and Sportsmedicine* 16, no. 3 (March 1988): 213-18.

Enoka, Roger M. *Neuromechanical Basis of Kinesiology.* Champaign, IL: Human Kinetics Publishers, Inc., 1988.

Fox, Edward L., and Donald K. Mathews. *The Physiological Basis of Physical Education and Athletics.* 3d ed. Philadelphia: Saunders College Publishing, 1981.

Fox, Edward L. *Sports Physiology.* 2d ed. Philadelphia: Saunders College Publishing, 1979.

Goldman, Robert M., Patricia Bush and Ronald Klatz. *Death in the Locker Room.* South Bend, IN: Icarus Press, 1984.

Guthrie, Helen A. *Introductory Nutrition.* 5th ed. St. Louis: The C. V. Mosby Company, 1983.

Hafen, Brent Q. *Nutrition, Food and Weight Control.* expanded ed. Boston: Allyn and Bacon, Inc., 1981.

Horrigan, Joseph and David Shaw. "Plyometrics: The Dangers of Depth Jumps." *High Intensity Training Newsletter* 2, no. 4 (Winter 1990): 15-21.

Jones, Arthur. *Nautilus Training Principles,* Bulletin #1. DeLand, FL: Nautilus Sports/Medical Industries, 1970.

———. "Specificity in Strength Training . . . The Facts and the Fables." *Athletic Journal* 57, no. 9 (May 1977): 70-75.

Jones, Arthur et al. *Safe, Specific Testing and Rehabilitative Exercise of the Muscles of the Lumbar Spine.* Santa Barbara, CA: Sequoia Communications, 1988.

Kennedy, Paul M. "What Determines Strength Potential?" *Scholastic Coach* 56, no. 2 (September 1986): 58-60.

King, B. G., and M. J. Showers. *Human Anatomy and Physiology.* 6th ed. Philadelphia: W. B. Saunders Co., 1969.

Leistner, Ken E. "A Brief Word on Plyometrics." *The Steel Tip* 3, no. 2 (February 1987): 1-2.

Mannie, Ken. "Strength Training Follies: The All-P.U.B. Team." *High Intensity Training Newsletter* 2, no. 2 (Summer 1990): 11-12.

Naismith, James. "Basket Ball." *American Physical Education Review* 19 (May 1914): 339-351.

NCAA Committee on Competitive Safeguards and Medical Aspects of Sports. "Ergogenic Aids and Nutrition." Overland Park, KS: NCAA memorandum, August 6, 1992.

Peterson, James A., ed. *Total Fitness: The Nautilus Way.* West Point, NY: Leisure Press, 1978.

Pipes, Thomas V. "A.C.T. - The Steroid Alternative." *Scholastic Coach* 57, no. 6 (January 1988): 106, 108-109, 112.

_____. *The Steroid Alternative.* Placerville, CA: Sierra Gold Graphics, 1989.

Riley, Daniel P. *Maximum Muscular Fitness: How To Develop Strength Without Equipment.* West Point, NY: Leisure Press, 1982.

_____. "Speed of Exercise Versus Speed of Movement." *Scholastic Coach* 48, no. 10 (May/June 1979): 90, 92-93, 97-98.

_____. *Strength Training by the Experts.* 2d ed. West Point, NY: Leisure Press, 1982.

_____. "Time and Intensity: Keys to Maximum Strength Gains." *Scholastic Coach* 50, no. 4 (November 1980): 65-66, 74-75.

Sage, George H. *Introduction to Motor Behavior: A Neuropsychological Approach.* 2d ed. Reading, MA: Addison-Wesley Publishing Company, 1977.

Schmidt, Richard A. *Motor Skills.* New York: Harper & Row, 1975.

Strauss, Richard H., ed. *Sports Medicine.* Philadelphia: W. B. Saunders Company, 1984.

Westcott, Wayne L. "Integration of Strength, Endurance and Skill Training." *Scholastic Coach* 55, no. 10 (May/June 1986): 74.

Wikgren, Scott. "The Plyometrics Debate." *Coaching Women's Basketball* 1, no. 5 (May/June 1988): 10-13.

Wilmore, Jack H. *Training For Sport And Activity: The Physiological Basis Of The Conditioning Process.* 2d ed. Boston: Allyn and Bacon, Inc., 1982.

Wolf, Michael D. "Health & Fitness Equipment Buying Guide." *Consumers Digest* 30, no. 5 (September/October 1991): 33-44.

ABOUT THE AUTHORS

Shaun Brown received his Bachelor of Science degree in Physical Education from Canisius College (NY) and his Master's degree in Exercise Physiology from Ohio State. He has been the Strength and Conditioning Coach at the University of Kentucky since April 1992. Coach Brown's primary responsibility is to develop and administer strength and conditioning programs for the men's and women's basketball teams. Previously, he served four years as the Strength and Conditioning Coach at Providence College. His coaching resume also includes stints at the University of Virginia, Ohio State, and Rutgers University.

Matt Brzycki received his Bachelor of Science degree in Health and Physical Education from Penn State. He has been the Strength and Conditioning Coach, Health Fitness Coordinator, and Nautilus Director at Princeton University since August 1990. His responsibilities include developing classes for the Physical Education curriculum along with training and evaluating the Physical Education and Nautilus Instructors. Coach Brzycki also teaches strength training classes for the students, faculty, and staff at Princeton University. He developed the Strength Training Theory and Applications class for Exercise Science and Sports Studies majors at Rutgers University and has taught the course since March 1990. Prior to entering college, he served four years in the United States Marine Corps including a tour of duty as a Drill Instructor. This is his second book.

GET INTO THE GAME!

FIVE-STAR BASKETBALL

Edited by Ed Schilling and Howard Garfinkel

Join the audience of some of the greatest lectures in the history of the legendary Five-Star basketball camp. Superstar coaches such as Bob Knight, Chuck Daly, Rick Pitino, George Raveling and Mike Fratello, as well as former star players such as Clark Kellogg and Johnny Newman, share insights and advice that not only will improve basketball skills but help anyone achieve his or her potential on and off the court.

```
224 pages • 7 X 10
0-940279-58-4 • $14.95
b/w photos
paper
```

SPALDING BASKETBALL INBOUND ATTACK

Tom Reiter

The most complete (and only) collection of out-of-bounds plays ever assembled! Accompanied by easy-to-follow diagrams, these effective plays will enhance the performance of teams at any level of play. The more than one hundred plays are supplemented by winning strategies for various special game situations.

```
128 pages • 7 X 10
0-940279-60-6 • $12.95
diagrams
paper
```

**All Masters Press titles,
including those in the Spalding Sports Library,
are available at bookstores or by calling
(800) 722-2677.
Catalogs are available upon request.**

COACHING BASKETBALL

The Official Centennial Volume of the National Association of Basketball Coaches

Edited by Jerry Krause

The ultimate reference book for all basketball coaches, this is the compilation of more than 130 articles by the nation's leading coaches at the professional, college, and high school levels. No coach who takes his or her job seriously should be without it!

Includes the following chapters:

- The Birth of the Game (James Naismith)
- Thoughts on Coaching (Al McGuire)
- Daily Practice (John Wooden)
- Organization of Practice and Season (Chuck Daly)
- Timeouts and Substitutions (Dean Smith)
- Tips on Scouting (Rick Majerus)
- Anatomy of a Rebound (George Raveling)
- Post Play (John Thompson)
- Zone Attacks (Jud Heathcote)
- Pressing Principles (Jerry Tarkanian)
- Match-up Press Defense (Rick Pitino)
- A Game Plan (Bob Knight)

> 384 pages • 8½ X 11
> 0-940279-29-0 • $24.95
> diagrams throughout
> cloth

FIVE-STAR BASKETBALL DRILLS

Edited by Howard Garfinkel

Includes 131 of the best conditioning and skill drills from Five-Star, the nation's premier basketball camp. A star-studded galaxy of coaches, including Mike Krzyzewski, Rick Pitino, and Bob Knight, share the activities that have proven successful year after year at Five-Star.

> 256 pages • 7 X 10
> 0-940279-22-3 • $14.95
> fully illustrated
> paper

MASTERS PRESS

DEAR VALUED CUSTOMER,

Masters Press is dedicated to bringing you timely and authoritative books for your personal and professional library. As a leading publisher of sports and fitness books, our goal is to provide you with easily accessible information on topics that interest you written by the most qualified authors. You can assist us in this endeavor by checking the box next to your particular areas of interest.

We appreciate your comments and will use the information to provide you with an expanded and more comprehensive selection of titles.

Thank you very much for taking the time to provide us with this helpful information.

Cordially,
Masters Press

Areas of interest in which you'd like to see Masters Press publish books:

☐ COACHING BOOKS
   Which sports? What level of competition?

☐ INSTRUCTIONAL/DRILL BOOKS
   Which sports? What level of competition?

☐ FITNESS/EXERCISE BOOKS
   ☐ Strength—Weight Training
   ☐ Body Building
   ☐ Other

☐ REFERENCE BOOKS
   what kinds?

☐ BOOKS ON OTHER
   Games, Hobbies
   or Activities

Are you more likely to read a book or watch a video-tape to get the sports information you are looking for?

I'm interested in the following sports as a participant:

I'm interested in the following sports as an observer:

Please feel free to offer any comments or suggestions to help us shape our publishing plan for the future.

Name _____ Age _____

Address _____

City _____ State _____ Zip _____

Daytime phone number _____

BUSINESS REPLY MAIL

FIRST CLASS MAIL   PERMIT NO. 1317   INDIANAPOLIS IN

POSTAGE WILL BE PAID BY ADDRESSEE

MASTERS PRESS

2647 WATERFRONT PKY EAST DR

INDIANAPOLIS IN 46209-1418

CONDITIONING FOR

Basketball

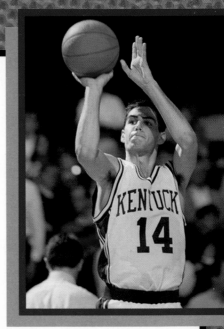

Advance praise for
Conditioning for **Basketball:**

"As a coach, I've felt very strongly about the importance of strength and conditioning as a way of preventing injury and improving a player's potential to excel. This book is easy-to-read yet loaded with information that satisfies the concerns I have for my players' conditioning."

Rick Pitino / Head Basketball Coach
The University of Kentucky Wildcats

"Conditioning for Basketball is the most comprehensive book ever written about strength and conditioning for basketball. It belongs in the hands of anyone who is involved with the strength training and conditioning of basketball players."

Mickey Marotti / Strength Coach
The University of Cincinnati Bearcats

"Being a professional basketball player, I know the value of proper conditioning. *Conditioning for Basketball* contains everything you need to know about preparing yourself to compete above the rim!"

Kenny "Sky" Walker
1989 NBA Slam Dunk Champ

"This book is must reading for coaches and players of all ages. I was particularly pleased to find that the authors didn't ignore the special needs of female athletes."

Mark Asanovich / Strength Coach
Anoka High School (MN)
1992 Class AA State Basketball Champs

"I liked it. The book is sharp and perceptive, attuned to what I call *the new world approach to strength training.*"

Herman L. Masin / Editor
Scholastic Coach Magazine

ISBN 0-940279-56-8
51295

SPORTS	$12.95
ISBN	0-940279-56-8

9 780940 279568